Words of Wisdom

For Everyday Living

Also by Andrew Hain and Helen W A Hain:

Living the Spiritual Laws
for Health and Abundance

Words of Wisdom

for Everyday Living

Andrew Hain and
Helen W A Hain

Well Within Therapies

Published by
Well Within Therapies
26 Orchard Road
Kingston upon Thames
KT1 2QW
Telephone 020 8549 1784

Disclaimer
Every care is taken to ensure that the routines, methods and processes that are set out herein are suitable to individuals of all levels of fitness. However, please note that such material may not be suitable for all. If you have any doubts, seek medical advice prior to commencement. Cease the programme immediately should you experience any discomfort and seek medical advice.

British Library Cataloguing-in-Publication Data
A catalogue record for this book is available from the British Library

ISBN 0-9545446-1-7

Printed and bound by CPI Antony Rowe, Eastbourne

Contents

33. One candle can light many others. Share your light with those who need it.
34. Every act is a choice: you always have an option.
35. Be guided by your Higher Self, not by your Ego
36. Intentions are important. What are your intentions for today?
37. Life is like a see saw: it needs both ups and downs.
38. A calm pond gives clear reflections. How is your pond?
39. Make today a special day because once it has gone you can't relive it.
40. A gift from the heart brings joy to the giver as well as to the receiver
41. Don't stumble in the dark when you can switch on the light
42. If you are balanced within the ups and downs in life won't get you down
43. Don't bear grudges: put peace in their place
44. Never interfere with another's journey: you don't know their destination.
45. A river is fed from its source: where does your nourishment come from?
46. Amid noise you can still find peace. In nothingness you can find everything
47. Choose your thoughts as carefully as you choose your words
48. Getting to know yourself isn't easy but the rewards are great
49. Have peace in your thoughts and this is what the world will reflect back to you
50. If you have doubts and fears you have lost trust in the Universe

Epilogue Spiritual Progression

Preface

This book has taken many years to complete. It began simply with the headings which Helen produced and entitled "Words of Wisdom". These short statements were designed to be printed on slips of paper or cards, with a view to selecting one at random and meditating upon it to give insight as to why the message was relevant for that particular moment. From time to time Helen felt inspired to add further to these words and channelled a few paragraphs on each of the statements from the Higher Realms. Often, this channelling would come through at unexpected times and places. Sometimes the words came to inspire and guide during times of difficulty and emotional low.

Still, the work lay dormant, resting in limbo whilst Helen decided how best to bring it to a wider audience. Then the Universe intervened and we experienced all sorts of problems, health and work related. It was amazing how similar our work problems were, even although we were employed in entirely different fields. The Universe was telling us that it was not the right time for "Words of Wisdom". However, our experiences during this period, and the guidance received from Higher Realms, led to us writing "Living the Spiritual Laws" which we published in 2003.

Again, the Universe has intervened to remind us of "Words of Wisdom" and the need to develop it further. This led to Andrew getting involved because the inspiration was to keep the format of "Living the Spiritual Laws", which meant that each of us channelled information on the statements. During this process further statements were given to us.

So what started with simple mottoes underwent another transformation and the results are published in this book (with a second book to follow).

We are both truly grateful for all our life experiences and relationships, and the learnings that have emerged from them. The experiences we have been through, the tears we have shed, have been an enormous contribution to our spiritual progression and we are particularly indebted to everyone who has been involved, including our children, parents, employers, friends, colleagues, to name but a few. We have been to many courses in colleges and universities but the greatest and most valuable lessons have come in the most unexpected ways. There have been many occasions when we have felt hurt, anger, jealousy, fear, resentment, rejection. We have blamed others for these feelings. We also know we have meted out these negative feelings in return, and held on to situations for too long.

We know we cannot change what has been said or done but we do know we have learned and gained immeasurable wisdom from these emotions. Without these situations we could not have reached the depths of despair to which one has to go in order to understand and grow. It is easy to love when all is going well but in such circumstances one cannot really comprehend what unconditional love truly is. Neither can one learn that one is responsible for one's own reactions and feelings. From the bottom of our hearts we thank everyone who has given the interactions and circumstances which have enabled us to experience who we really are, and who we can really be. Without them all, this book would never have been written. All we ask is that those who read it may find they can identify with its contents and find the encouragement to move forward spiritually. The events in our lives seem to prove beyond doubt that everyone is an Angel in disguise. Thank you Angels for helping us to remember our Divine connection. Truly, All is One, and One is All.

We ask that you use this book when you seek inspiration and upliftment. Dip into it at random after taking a few moments quiet during which you have asked for guidance from your Higher Self.

At the end of the channelling of each motto we have selected what we consider to be a key statement to summarise what the channellings reveal. We have also added questions to encourage you to go within yourself and find your own spiritual answers.

Remember to consider what you read, and only take on ideas you are comfortable with. You have the free will, therefore you make the choice.

AH & HWAH

1. Love your enemies: they are your greatest teachers

Tests are sent to give you the opportunity to demonstrate your God-like qualities. You are given difficult situations and relationships to see how you deal with them. It is easy to love and be grateful and caring when your needs are met and everything is harmonious. However, to appreciate what gifts you have, you need to experience the opposite end of the scale. To appreciate love you have to know what it feels like to be unloved. To appreciate plenty you have to know what it feels like to be deprived.

Be grateful for every person you interact with and every experience you encounter. These are opportunities to experience all things and find balance in your life. When people react in a way which upsets you, think about why you are feeling upset or even angry. Delve inwards and bring forth God-like qualities such as love, understanding, fearlessness, and see the power when these qualities are utilised. Thank the other person for being an Angel in disguise who has given you the opportunity to demonstrate who you really are.

Enemies are here defined as people you do not get along with very well. You don't have to have a pitched battle with someone to make them your enemy. Perhaps enemy is not quite the right word: it's the people you tend to shun and treat like an "enemy", and keep out of your life.

It is nice to have a group of friends around you: people with the same interests and views as yourself. What a jolly bunch you are. But will they tell you the bad things that you try to ignore? No, they will not upset you and will, in all probability, reinforce whatever it is you want to believe about yourself.

However, from a developmental viewpoint, this does not help you. Ego has taken over your Being and you only want to hear what your Ego is saying to you.

Your enemies, on the other hand, will tell you exactly how they see you. They will tell you all those things that you really don't want to hear because Ego is fooling you. Ego wants your mind closed. Ego wants you to live the life that it has determined for you. Ego is a selfish aspect in this respect.

Listen to what Ego says you don't want to hear. There will be truth in the words that are directed at you. Deep down you probably know this, but you are fighting hard to ignore it because Ego demands it.

If you want to grow spiritually or personally, if you want to develop your Being then you need to be open minded and listen to what everyone says. After that, consult your Inner Self and consider everything that has occurred. Only then can you arrive at a true conclusion. It's true: "you can fool some of the people some of the time, but not all of the people all of the time".

You can fool yourself by acting according to Ego but your enemies can see beyond the veil and know the truth.

They have much to teach you, you should listen more often.

You are given difficult situations and relationships to see how you deal with them.

Think of a recent difficult situation. How did you react?

Could you invoke more spiritual qualities to deal with a similar event in the future?

With whom did you interact today?

What "home truths" did you hear?

2. A cloudy sky doesn't mean the sun isn't shining.

It is easy to forget about the sun on dull, cloudy days. We think there is no sun but it is always there shining down on the earth even although its rays may be temporarily obscured by clouds. We moan and groan, complaining about the lack of sunshine and forget about the importance of the clouds and the rain they bring for our survival.

When we go through difficult times we forget the good times and focus on the problems, becoming submerged in the negative aspects. We find it hard to understand the good behind them, but we must look at what these problems and experiences bring us. Just as the sun and rain bring growth, our experiences bring us spiritual growth and understanding. Instead of complaining, thank the Universe for the opportunity for growth and see yourself blossom for having experienced what at first seemed nothing but an obstacle to peace and joy.

Even on a cloudy day the light will shine. It may be somewhat diffused, but there is more than enough to be able to see clearly. The clouds in a sense are obstacles. They can be likened to bad situations. Sometimes they bring rain, sometimes they blow over quickly. If you look at clouds they never stay in the same shape for very long. Neither do they remain in the same place, although some days there are so many that you may perceive them as unmoving. But always the sun is shining behind them: how else could you "see" the cloud?

If you travel on an aeroplane and climb above the cloud base you can see blue skies and sunshine. So too with your problems and bad situations. If you see them as unmoving they will get darker and darker, and drop their rain upon you. Your problems will get you down, if you let them. However, you have a choice. You can rise above them or you can take action to change their shape and motion and thus disperse them. Either way you get clear blue skies and sunshine.

Some situations require action, and you should take it appropriately. Others, when looked at, will turn out to be not as serious as first thought and can be left alone.

Whatever the case, always look for the positive. Always look for the lesson. Ask yourself what this is teaching you. If you need to take action, do it with love and understanding. The more you do so the sooner the light will come flooding through and your cloud will be gone. Always remember that, no matter how bad you perceive a problem to be, the answer lies behind it, and, with your positive attitude, you will see it shine through.

Whatever the case, always look for the positive.

Do you find it hard to be positive when an event isn't what you'd like it to be?

If so, what actions or attitudes can you adopt to see it through?

Did you have any problems today?

If so, what experiences did they bring?
What did you learn?

3. Do your best today and tomorrow you'll be satisfied with yesterday

Use your time wisely each day. Take time to meditate and plan how to get the best from the time you have available. Then get on with what is right, and be prepared to accept the outcome knowing that whatever you chose to do was the right choice. Whatever you have to do each day, make it important. See its place in your plan even if it's a task you have to do rather than something you do because you feel drawn to it.

Short breaks during which you go into the quiet will keep you on course. By the end of the day you will have achieved what you planned and tomorrow will bring you satisfaction when you look back. In the past you have often looked back and been filled with regret and were angry with yourself for not achieving, or for not having succeeded. These feelings then fill your mind and prevent you from progressing. Instead of having wasted only yesterday you set yourself up to fail again. Do your best today, and tomorrow the good feelings will be with you, giving you the momentum to do your best yet again.

Every day we should be doing whatever we need to do to the best of our ability. It is true to say that if something is worth doing it should be done well.

How can anyone be satisfied with a job that's been poorly executed? As a consumer we get upset and angry at shoddy workmanship and we complain until we get compensation or the matter put right. If this doesn't happen we vow never to use those services again, and tell our friends of our experience.

As the person doing the job, what is there to gain from not doing it properly? Is a bad reputation really worth it? Do you get any satisfaction from a shoddy performance?

If you put your heart into every task you have to do you will be sending out love to the Universe. You will be raising the positive energy levels all around, and we know that what goes round comes round. Therefore that love you give out in doing a job to the best of your ability will come back to you and raise your levels.

Also it's good to know that when you look back on what you did you can do so with pride and satisfaction because you know you did your best. You didn't try to cheat. You only get positive responses when you do it well.

Can you imagine what it would be like to know that each day you will have a great positive feeling, one of self satisfaction in what you do and have done. As with everything else, you only get out of it what you put in. So when you give your all you get the maximum return. What a lovely feeling!

Do your best today

Did you give of your best in everything you were involved in today?

Was there anything you could have done better?

4. If you cling too tightly to what you love you're more likely to lose it

Whatever you love or indeed whoever you love, love all unconditionally. Do not make claims to anything or anybody. The Universe will give you whatever you need and it may be taken from you if there is a lesson to learn, or if you no longer have a need. You may think you have a need but you cannot see the entire picture so do not rely on your own judgment.

Trust your needs will be met and the right experiences will appear. By clinging to something you think is vital you are not only losing trust in the Universe but you are trying to set up conditions which may not be in your best interests in the long run. By clinging to something you are building up fear of losing it, and these negative emotions will give off negative energies which will bring about what you are trying to avoid happening.

Energy has to move, and you need to remember it has to flow in order to give and receive. If you fail to give and share you will fail to receive. Fear of losing something focuses your attention on one area and you neglect other aspects of your life. By clinging to something you don't just run the risk of losing it but you lose out on other aspects of your life as well.

Don't set up conditions. Accept what you have with gratitude. Fearful emotions will only attract fear. Remind yourself of the abundance the Universe has given you, knowing that even if circumstances change, you will still be blessed with your needs being met.

My friend, this is true. What you will succeed in doing is to strangle that which you love and end up with something lifeless. You will, by your actions, squeeze the very lifeblood from it and it will wither and die. By all means love it, care for it, admire it, but do not stifle it with your overbearing attention and control. Whilst you may think you are acting with the best of intentions you will be depriving it of what it needs most of all: to express its free will, or its ability to develop and grow.

You should not try to exert control on anyone or anything. You can offer words of guidance, express personal experiences, make suggestions, but you must not expect to control whoever or whatever. You are responsible only for your own thoughts, words and actions, and should realise that everything else and everyone else has a similar responsibility to itself, themselves.

If you start to cling so tightly then you are forming too great an attachment and when the inevitable breakdown occurs you will be badly hurt.

By being too overbearing you are allowing your Ego to take over. Ease back and be guided by your Higher Self, your Inner Being.

Whatever or whoever you feel this love for, be free to express it. Expressions of love are a positive force and do so much good in so many ways. However, you must also allow whatever you love the room and the will to develop in its own way. True love means allowing freedom. With that freedom comes growth, and with that growth love will return to you in magnified quantities.

Love all unconditionally.

What are you clinging to?

What is the worst that could happen if you lost it?

5. A friend is someone you don't know until you're in trouble

It is always easy to be a friend to someone who has no specific needs and demands nothing of you. However it is only when you experience a crisis that you find out how willing your so called friends are to be of assistance. It is important to still send out love to those who avoid you in your time of need, but remember to ask for help and you will be amazed that it usually comes from the most unlikely persons. You will see goodness and love come from where you never expected it to be.

Be grateful and give thanks. Always be positive, knowing that the Universe will care for you in unexpected ways. Remember the Law of Giving, and be the Angel of Love to others whom you perhaps do not know and whom you may never meet again. Being a friend for a few moments may mean more to someone than a host of acquaintances who don't want to know the person when help is required. A friend in need may be an Angel in disguise.

We, all of us, have a circle of people we call friends. We socialise, we spend time together. We laugh, we chat, and we have good times together. After all that's what friends are for, isn't it?

Well, yes, to an extent. It is good to enjoy the company of others, especially those whose interests and outlook are similar to our own and we can have a good time. However, like just about anything else, friends can be categorised according to criteria and we use labels such as "casual acquaintance" or "very old friend" to distinguish between people with whom we have any sort of relationship.

But how do you tell "true friends" from "fair weather friends"? On the surface you cannot, and this is an excellent reminder that you cannot judge if you do not possess all the facts. As the Universe besets you with tests, so too must you test the depth of friendship. It's a rocky path to travel, but the journey is worthwhile because you will know who your fellow travellers truly are.

It's been said elsewhere in these channellings that adversity comes to teach, not destroy, and it is usually in such times that you will travel the narrow difficult path of discovering who really is / are your true friend(s).

Someone who will put out for you. Someone who will give you the help, support and encouragement you need. Someone who will walk in the darkness with you, bringing their light to bear upon your troubles. Someone who will share your burden voluntarily and without complaint.

Often, too, the discovery of who your friend is will come as a surprise. Yes, there will have been "obvious" candidates but how will you react when a different answer comes? With joy and exultation we would hope.

The difficulty with trouble is that it can prove you wrong. Why? Because you had made decisions without having all the facts. Always be open to change. People change. They come and they go, and your circle of friends will change as you change. Sometimes people reappear in your circle after countless years, and when you take the time to discover why, you will be amazed at the stories they have to tell.

Everyone's journey is important and so it is important for us to find companions who can be relied upon to step the path with us.

In concluding we would like to ask how you fare as a friend to those in your circle. Would you support them in a crisis? Really? Truly? Honestly?

Be the Angel of Love to others

Who helped, supported and encouraged you in your time of need?

Did you give any energy back to the Universe by way of helping someone else?

When was the last time you helped a complete stranger who was in trouble?

6. If you stop thinking positively you might as well give up

When you are beset by problems, seeing yourself sinking in deeper with no hope of improvement, you are giving in to the situation and giving up hope and trust that events will change. Negative thinking, loss of faith and trust will keep attracting what you wish to eradicate from your life. No matter what, remember things change as energy is always in motion.

Raise up your level of consciousness to your Soul and bring in the trust that all will be well. Send out positive energies believing you are abundant. You will attract what it is you desire, but make sure that what you desire is for the highest good for yourself and anyone else involved.

Stay positive, stay focussed, believe in yourself and in your ability to create your reality. Give up the negative thinking which will adversely affect your spiritual growth, be thankful for what you have and welcome what comes to you. Appreciate what you are learning and look forward to the next opportunity for growth.

You know that your journey along your spiritual pathway is never easy, that is why some of you will not tread it. You may be able to avoid your spiritual commitment, but you certainly cannot avoid living the physical life.

But here, too, the pathway is not even. There are ups and downs, there are places where the going is tough, yet you choose to walk this pathway in preference to your real life plan. That is your choice.

When you are beset with difficulties, on either pathway, how do you cope? How do you deal with the objects that block your way forward? You will know that nothing ever runs as smoothly as you plan it or perceive it to unfold.

These obstacles come for a reason: they come to teach you a lesson, they come to bring you a message or an insight. Is that how you see them? Or do you rant and rave about the blockage? Do you get yourself into a panic or dark mood because all is not as well as you want it to be?

We have told you many times that however you react, that emotion echoes round the Universe and is amplified: then it comes back to you.

Your emotions put you into a spiral: you can travel upwards or downwards. It all depends on you.

Our message to you is to stop and look for the message: learn from the situation. Look for the positive in the event and apply it. There is always positivity to be found; sometimes you need to look deeply for it.

Positivity will carry you upwards, emotionally. It will give you a boost. It will develop you as a person. With positivity you will have an inner knowing that you will achieve.

If you take the other view then you can only take yourself down emotionally, and you will sink deeper into the depths. That is why, if you stop being positive, you should stop altogether, for the only way left for you is down.

Believe in yourself and in your ability to create your reality

How do you deal with problems? Bottle them up? Ignore them? Take positive action?

Do you look for reasons, lessons, and messages when problems appear?

What assistance / support / tools / skills do you need to help you through?

Where will you find these?

7. If you lose sight of the goal posts you can't score

There are often times when you complain of being in a rut and not moving forward and enjoying success. How can you move forward if you have no destination to reach. It is vital to set goals and to make sure they are realistic. Be sure they will give you true satisfaction and do not set goals for the wrong reasons. Don't be influenced by others, don't go for something because of the financial rewards or status that could be enjoyed.

Examine what you really want and be guided by your heart. Does it feel right? Is it in tune with your spiritual aspirations? Be sure of what you really wish to attain. Ask for guidance in your meditations and await a response. Believe in yourself and take steps to go forward. Write down what you want to achieve and use affirmations to fill your unconscious mind with positive thoughts. This ensures the goal posts are always in your vision.

If you lose sight of them you could be going round in circles as if in a maze, continually facing blockages and moving around using lots of energy only to find you are close to your starting point, having failed to progress as planned. Visualise the goal posts and head for them with determination, knowing that when you get there you will have achieved your goal.

A sporting metaphor! In many sports there are goal posts which are the target of a team's ambitions. The game is won by the team who puts the ball or whatever between the goal posts most often.

In everyday life you set yourself lots of targets. There are many things you want to achieve. To help you do so you break down each ambition into manageable pieces and call them goals.

You work towards each goal and as you achieve it you feel a sense of wellbeing. You are making progress. However there are many distractions waiting to push or pull you off your path, or to act as barriers across your path.

They can set you back quite considerably and cause you pain and stress. So long as you keep your goal posts in sight you have a good chance of achieving. Once you let distractions stray across your path your sight of the goal posts becomes blocked, or, worse still, they disappear from view. If you don't know exactly where the goal is how can you "score"?

Distractions come to test you. They come to see if your resolve is strong. They come to see if you really want to walk the narrow path. They come to determine how focussed you are, how committed you really are.

This applies equally well to your spiritual goals. Have you set any? Well, actually, yes you have. You set them before you were born. You came into this world with a set of spiritual goals already in place.

Perhaps you have forgotten your spiritual goals? To find them you need to consult your Higher Self. Your Higher Self will be able to remind you why you are here and who you really are.

Even if you have remembered your spiritual goals you should be consulting with your Higher Self on a very regular basis. By doing this you will find out how well you are progressing. By doing this you will be keeping the goal posts in sight.

As with all the goals you set yourself it is good to be able to take time out with a mentor who can give an honest assessment and assured advice. Your Higher Self is the best mentor you will ever have and will provide for your needs. Undoubtedly you will score highly if you seek out your true mentor.

Distractions come to test you

Do you feel distractions divert you from your pathway, leaving you in a rut? If so, can you see a way out?

Do you set yourself goals? If not, how will you know when you make any progress?

8. Life is like the seasons: there's always something new to look forward to.

Nature doesn't remain static. There is motion you cannot see which moves the plant or tree to the next stage of growth. Each season brings beauty and colour, and is necessary for future development to take place.

Take time to look back over events in your life, noting even what seemed insignificant at the time. You will be amazed at the connections there were between events. Without all the links you wouldn't be what you are today.

See your life cycle in this way. Each step is a preparation for the next one. Some things blossom and grow, other things blossom and die in order for new things to move in and replace them. Whatever fades away had a purpose even if you didn't realise it at the time. Every piece of a jigsaw is necessary to complete the picture. See your life as one big picture and look forward to the next piece of the jigsaw to aid its completion.

You live in a physical world in which nature pervades. Even in your "concrete jungles" you will find nature building an environment. You will find plants growing in all sorts of strange and unexpected locations: you will find life in countless places where you perhaps did not think it could survive. Such is the glory of nature.

Because the Earth, your physical world, lies at an angle to the Sun, most of the planet experiences seasons. For example, in the UK you get a cold season, a warm season, and in between them two temperate seasons.

Life on Earth is therefore cyclic, as nature changes with the coming and going of each season. Thus there are always new things to anticipate, events to watch out for. When does the first daisy appear on your lawn? When do some birds migrate for the coming winter?

How is your personal life related to nature and the seasons? Possibly more than you realise, with the reasonably obvious response that you take your holidays in the warmest season, although with accessible world wide travel available that may no longer be the case in every instance.

Do you live your life in a mundane fashion? Do you do the same things day in, day out all year round? Do you follow the herd? How much joy and satisfaction does that bring you?

What if we suggested that you try different things? Would you consider it? Would you actually do it? Things like taking a different route to work, or an earlier or later train. Maybe even take the bus or walk, at least part of the way, instead. You would then have things to look forward to, instead of the same (boring) routine.

There are many things you could do instead of whatever it is you do now. Change your routine. Life on Earth is meant to be always changing. The seasons tell you that. Nature tells you that. Is it time to listen?

Do you live your life in a mundane fashion?

Do you look forward to every new day, seeing it as bringing something new and exciting to your life? Or is it a case of "same stuff, different day"?

Have you tried to make changes to your routine? If so, did you enjoy the experience?

Would you do it again?

9. The greatest gifts are already within: you've only got to unwrap them

Everyone is unique with his or her own special talents and abilities. How often do we see people who never unlock their abilities? They remain dormant, never being used to assist the individual or others who could benefit from them. So often energy is used up in negative ways: anger, fear and similar emotions. These absorb the individual's life, and time fritters away with nothing achieved except the attraction of more of what the person was trying to avoid.

Take time to examine your thoughts and how you spend your time and energy. Use these wisely. Gain control of your thinking. Still your thoughts and this will lead to communication with your Higher Self. This is the gateway to finding your true Self, your pathway and your special gifts that you have always had. Be grateful for what you have been given and use them in the right way.

We are spiritual beings operating out of a physical body. We live and interact with everyone and everything on the physical plane. Our view of our existence is necessarily almost exclusively limited to physical manifestations.

Sometimes we express our emotional and mental states to help us get our interaction understood. Sometimes our emotional and mental states take hold of us when things aren't going well for us or whenever something really touches us deep inside.

Do you ever cry tears of joy or genuine sadness? This happens when our emotional side has been involved. Whatever the event that has triggered our tears, we cry because we feel part of that event. We feel its sorrow or joy and we can't help but express ourselves. In a sense we have unwrapped a present from the Universe.

There are many more presents from the Universe waiting to be unwrapped. Because we live in the physical we rarely look at the other levels, especially our spiritual level. Emotions we are generally familiar with and often misinterpret their presence as weakness. Mental faculties are not used to their full potential by most people who tend to do things and go about their daily business in a mundane, almost non-thinking manner. As for our spiritual side, well, very few give it a second thought.

It is a sadness that we do not use our spiritual connection very often, if at all. We are all connected to Source. We are all part of Source. Everyone on the planet is connected through our spiritual side. All is one and one is All. Very few know this, fewer still respect it.

If only we would step back from the hurly-burly of the physical world where Ego clashes with Ego, where dogma dictates, and stress, pain and hurt abound. If only we would take time to sit in quiet contemplation and make that connection with our vital spark, how different we could be. Inside each of us are the Universe's gifts to us. Unwrap them and you will be surprised at what is there. Your life needn't be the hustle-bustle you have let it become.

You will discover peace, tranquillity, a life plan that you set out prior to birth. You will discover abundance, wisdom, guidance, help, and so much more. The spiritual gifts waiting for you to collect are individually so much more valuable than all the worldly physical gifts put together. They are yours, so open them up.

There are many more presents from the Universe waiting to be unwrapped.

Inside each of us there are spiritual gifts from the Universe.

What gifts or talents do you think lie waiting for you to unwrap and use?

Does this excite you?

10. Be a creator not a destroyer

There are many people who believe they have no control whatsoever over their own destiny. How often do you hear the lament "poor me" or "why do things happen to me?". This is the defeatist attitude of one who has given his or her power away to others. This is co dependence. It is allowing others to make you feel happy or sad. Realise the power of positive thinking. Thoughts are what build your reality. Give out negative thoughts and these will create a negative existence for you. Take control of your thoughts. Make them loving and pure, and what you give out is what will come back to you. There is no escape from the Law of Cause and Effect.

Being a creator is taking responsibility for your thoughts and actions. You will never realise the power to create until you use it and see the results. Whenever you are faced with a problem send thoughts of love, healing, forgiveness and you will be amazed at how these thoughts can turn around situations which seemed would never change. Make sure that what you create is what you really want.

By allowing guidance from your Higher Self to build your reality you will feel positive and be joyful. You will be creating in accordance with the Spiritual Laws. However, by being guided by your Ego what you build will have no substance. Whatever good intentions you have, they will be destroyed by the passion of the Ego absorbed with material gain. Do not destroy the opportunities for progress, but take every moment and use it to create love in your life.

It is easier to destroy than to build. It is easier to descend than ascend. It is easier to be negative than positive. Take the challenge of the harder route for its rewards are greater. You will need to use your imagination, your inherent skills and your creativity to walk the road less travelled.

Each of us is born with creativity. Many of us deny we have it, many of us refuse to use it, and many believe they have lost it. We all have it, right through our lives, so look for it and use it.

Creativity knows no bounds in use. Every tool you use is the result of someone's creativity. How many times have you said "I wish I had thought of that"? The sad part is that you didn't because your creativity was "missing". Every work of art, whether you like it or not, has resulted from someone's creativity. When was the last time you used yours?

Destruction, on the other hand, is far easier. Pull it apart, take it to pieces, ruin it. All that energy is used in negative action. We do it as if it was second nature to us. It is an automatic reaction sometimes. Indeed it is almost a defensive action. But need it be so? Should we take delight in destroying what someone else has striven to create?

We should look for the positive in everything instead of applying the negative in a mindless act. Look for the lesson or meaning in what we crave to destroy and build positively on it. If we each were to act positively think how much wonderful, positive energy we would give to the Universe. Think how much positive energy would circulate and what it would do for everyone. What a wonderful creation.

There is no escape from the Law of Cause and Effect.

With this in mind ....
What would you like to give out?
What do you think you should avoid giving out?

When did you last use your creativity?

What feelings did you have at its completion?

11. If you can't find peace in your heart you won't find it anywhere

Do not look to others for peace of mind, happiness or security. Others are not responsible for your emotions and are not there to ensure your wellbeing. All have free will and you can choose how you feel and how you react to circumstances that present themselves to you. No matter what happens you can choose your reaction. This is not a responsibility to be given to others. Appreciate the free will you have and choose wisely.

Close your eyes and remind yourself of a time when you felt totally at peace. Allow this feeling to flow from your heart and totally encompass you. Peace cannot be accessed unless you trust that it's ok to feel that way. To allow peace to be with you, you have to know that no matter what is happening to you or around you everything is just right for what you need to learn.

By all means offer love and support to others when they struggle. Don't try to take away learning situations from them. Stay peaceful and loving, and this will assist them to find these feelings within themselves. Peace within means you accept whatever external circumstances occur. Accept what you are given and peace will follow.

Where indeed do you find peace, but at the Source. You have to be at one with yourself before you can experience peace somewhere else. For how else will you recognise peace outwith if you do not have it, have not experienced it, within?

If you are in turmoil physically, mentally or emotionally you will never discover peace on a spiritual level.

There are places you may go where all seems still, calm and quiet, but you will not settle into it if you are a raging torrent inside.

If you have love in your heart you will begin to understand peace. Peace is more than just a sense of calmness or quietness. It doesn't have to be experienced in solitude either. When you have love for all things in your heart your whole being will find peace.

Peace comes when you are at one with everything and everybody. When you truly realise that you are part of everything and everything is part of you, a great spiritual peace will pervade your very being.

This peace will bring you joy, happiness, belonging. This peace will change you: will change your outlook, will change how you react to situations. In short this peace will change your life.

You have to go inside and make that communication. You have to commit to unconditional love, to giving and receiving, to stop making judgments on people and situations. When you can do this you will truly find peace. From your heart centre it will radiate outwards and everywhere you go, everywhere you look, you will find peace.

Peace comes when you are at one with everything and everybody.

When was the last time you felt totally at peace?

What actions could you take to ensure you could feel peaceful more often?

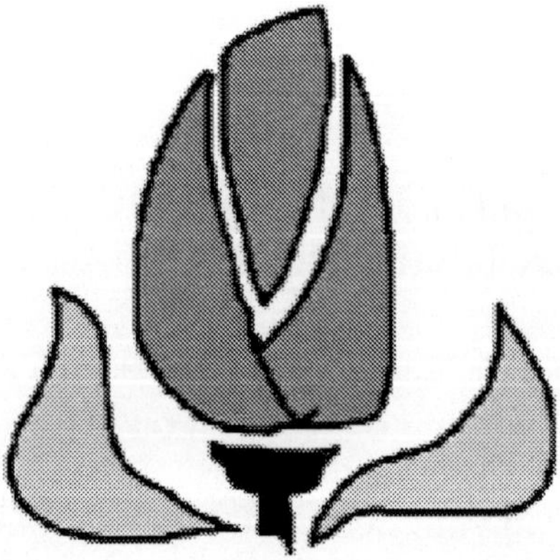

12. If you dwell on the past and worry about the future you miss out on the present

How much time have you wasted by crying over past events you could do nothing about, and how much time have you wasted fearing what the future might bring? You have no control over the past. You can't change what has happened but you can change your attitude towards it. This is taking control of the mind which wants to control you.

Take control of your thoughts. Let the past go and be in the present ready to move on. You can plan for the future but don't sit fearing what may never happen. Accept that you are doing your best in the present and enjoy it, be in control and prepare yourself for the future. Be ready to accept that whatever comes will be an opportunity for growth, and that if you ask for help you will be given the strength to get through. The present is continually moving into the past and the opportunity is gone for ever if you miss it.

Use your quiet times to be fully in the present. Ask for love and light to encompass you, and send these out to those around you. You can send these qualities into the past to heal it and project them into the future so that they will be there for you and others. This is being in control. This is showing trust that the Universe is caring for your needs. Be flexible, going with the flow of events, and your thoughts will be in the right place at the right time.

In terms of time there is only one place you should be and that is in the here and now. You really have to live in the moment because that is where your body is. It isn't in the past and it isn't in the future. It is here, now.

Why should you want to dwell on what has been and now is gone? Maybe you did something you now regret. Maybe someone has offended you. You cannot change what has been done: the action happened and cannot be changed. If you are to blame then you could apologise, send love, and then release the event. Your act of love will allow you to move on. If you are the victim then forgive, send love and move on.

Similarly, why do you want to worry about the future? What will be, will be. By all means plan for the future, but be prepared also to be flexible, for you may have to alter your plans in the light of how the present acts upon them. Will it rain tomorrow? Does it matter? If you are prepared for eventualities then there is no need to worry.

So, having released yourself from the past, and prepared yourself for the future, you are left exactly where the Universe wants you to be: in the present. This is where your life is and this is where you perform best. This is where your challenges are laid down and this is where you find success.

Yesterday has gone and has given you memories. Tomorrow, with its hopes has not arrived, so you must live for today. Today is the day you receive all your rewards.

You can't change what has happened but you can change your attitude towards it.

Are your thoughts frequently on past events? If so, why not let them go with love.

What draws you backwards in time?

What change in attitude do you have to make in order to free yourself from the past?

13. Don't cling to the present: it's always moving backwards

Live each day by being fully in it. Take what comes and be grateful for everything, even the situations which seem to create concern and unpleasantness. Deal with them as they arise in a loving way and be prepared to let them go and become part of your past whilst you continue to stay with the present.

If you face adversity with anger, resentment and hurt you are creating a link from which it is hard to cut loose. As the event moves further into the past you are still with it and find it hard to focus on new circumstances. Is it really worth being absorbed in events which happened a long time ago?

If this is how you deal with problems your burden will snowball and you will carry heavy baggage throughout your life. If you show love and acceptance for yourself and others you will be able to let go, move on and look forward to the future instead of looking back at the past with regret.

It is said that you should always live in the present because that's where you are. Live for the moment, live for the now. That is sound advice because it means you will live your life according to what is occurring right now.

You can make plans for the future, but, because it hasn't happened yet, you still need to be prepared to alter them. That's why you live in the present: to make these adjustments so that plans come to fruition.

Similarly, you cannot live in the past for it has gone and has been indelibly written. It cannot be changed. You can only learn from it and adjust accordingly.

So the one choice you have is the present. Live it to the full, enjoy each moment as it passes and take what you can from it. However, like all things to do with time, you cannot capture it or preserve it. It comes, it goes.

If you try to hang on to whatever has caught your attention then you will be laying down an anchor and you will be attached to the past, for that's what has become of your special moment.

As you move forwards, it moves backwards. Take the memories with you, but don't dwell on them. Don't pine for it when things change. Remember fondly and move on. Take the lesson with you as you travel forwards.

Learn from the past, plan for the future, but live in the present: it's the only place you can be.

Live each day by being fully in it.

See each day as a new beginning, a new opportunity for progression. In your journal note what you have learned during today, and let go of what will no longer serve you.

Do you ever take time to sit quietly, just watching the moment? Just observing, not thinking about it, not judging it, not getting involved in it.

If not, consider starting now and make it a habit.

14. If you see something you don't like you may be seeing part of yourself

The world around us is a reflection of our inner thoughts and desires. If we are at peace with our own being, fill ourselves with love and are satisfied with the way we are, we will see the same qualities around us and in others. If you are filled with fear, anger, dissatisfaction, sadness then that is what you are sending out to the world and those around you, and these are the qualities that will be reflected back to you.

If you smile at someone you are likely to get a smile back but if you scowl or shout at someone you are likely to get unpleasant reactions. Don't try to change others. Work on yourself and you will soon find the world is a better place. Develop the God-like qualities within yourself and you will be able to see the good within others.

In our physical existence we see lots of things: some we like, some we don't and some have a neutral impact on us. We are all different and so our likes and dislikes are different too. We make these judgments from knowledge and experience in the main although there are times we don't know why we like or dislike something: we get a "feeling".

It is perhaps when we get this "feeling" that we should make further enquiries of ourselves. Why do we get this feeling? What is it about our interaction with whatever that we like or dislike? Generally we get feelings about things we don't like.

We get cold shivers, we feel scared, we get a knot in our stomach. We can't explain it, but it happens. Why?

Are we seeing a reflection of ourself in the whatever? Is it an aspect of ourself that we don't like, and the whatever is reminding us of that? That's why we said earlier that further investigation is needed.

Is our Inner Self talking to us in these moments, telling us that we have deviated from our life plan, our spiritual mission? Do you know what your mission is? In times of creepy feelings it is intuition that is talking to you: intuition comes from your Inner Self.

Learn from your experiences and consult with your Inner Self. That way you will know that you are on the right path: the path you picked as the one to follow. Then the next time you see something you don't like you will know that until you do something about it, it will distract you from your real goal. Seeing something you don't like may remind you that you perhaps have something of that quality within yourself which is hindering your spiritual progression.

Develop the God-like qualities within yourself and you will be able to see the good within others.

Do you find it easy or difficult to see the God in others?

What feelings fill your being?

Which, if any, do you need to change?

How will you do that?

15. A hug may be all someone else needs

Your culture has taught you to keep a safe distance from others. You have been taught that everyone should be in his or her own space and that touch is taboo except in special circumstances eg. within families. Even so, many families find it difficult to hug or kiss each other.

Very often you cannot put into words what you want to say. You are frightened you make matters worse, say the wrong thing or that what you say is misinterpreted. Appropriate touch can say more than words and can be much more comforting to someone who is upset.

A hug shows you care and can mean so much to someone who is upset or lonely. People hug their pets but seem reluctant to hug friends. Follow your intuition and if a hug seems appropriate go ahead. If you are unsure you can always ask someone if they would like a hug or even hold their hand. There may be no words but this physical gesture will bring healing on other levels.

There are many occasions when we have seen a friend or family member who is feeling down or does not appear to be at the peak of their form. Well, that's the conclusion we reached and we have brashly stepped forward into the breach to give counsel, advice, offer all sorts of assistance. But really we haven't asked if it was wanted.

We have acted judgmentally and, good as our intentions are, we haven't helped at all. Indeed we have hindered or confused the matter by our action. Maybe we have also generated anger towards us from the person we were trying to help.

The situation can deteriorate rapidly because we then feel hurt when our offer of help is rejected or our advice is scorned.

You probably know what we are saying because our guess is that you too have been on the "wrong end" of unwanted and unsolicited advice and have felt outraged at the offer.

So, how best to deal with the situation? Unless we know all the facts we cannot make a judgment. Appearances, as you should know, can be deceptive. Usually things are not nearly as bad as we all make them seem. A gentle question or two will guide you in your wish to help or support.

Do not be upset if help is turned down. Perhaps your friend feels capable of solving whatever their problem is without outside assistance. Be glad for them. Show them how glad you are that they feel able to cope. Give them a hug: a great big warm hug.

That tells them you are sending out love. It tells them you are there for support if required. It tells them that you have faith and trust in their assessment of the situation. It will give them the confidence to tackle what they have to.

All our good intentions are best used in sending out love, in demonstrating love. Often, by keeping silent, we bring out the best in others. The hug is the action that says it all. That hug is so reassuring.

The hug is the action that says it all.

Make a list of those you hug.

Are there others in your life who may benefit from a hug?

How did you feel when you were last hugged?

16. Dissolve your problems with love

No matter what the problem is, we say apply the Law of Unconditional Love. Most people find this impossible to apply but if they would only give it a try they would realise it never fails to dissolve problems. There is fear of being out of control, of allowing others to control you and hurt you even more. There is a desire to fight back with demands and expectations.

Sending out unconditional love shows inner strength and a commitment to what you know to be true. The greatest power in the world is love and to show unconditional love is to allow this power to radiate from you to all life. Send love to people, places, events but there must be no conditions attached. Have no attachment to a particular outcome. Even when you are in pain physically or emotionally do not get angry or fight it. Love it for what it teaches you and ask for assistance and insight when you need this.

By constantly sending forth unconditional love, problems will not be viewed as problems but simply as another test on the pathway to enlightenment.

Problems. We always see problems as bad, as negative. We see problems as stumbling blocks, obstacles placed on our pathway to prevent progress. Problems are something bothersome to be overcome, sometimes at great personal cost.

Do we ever stop and wonder why we are at times beset with problems? Perhaps we are being tested for skills and traits. Perhaps the Universe is trying to tell us something. There must surely be a lesson to learn from the situation.

When we are beset by a problem we enter grumpy mode, because we are being delayed and are impatient to move ahead. We set about our problem solving with a distinct feeling of negativity. It's like a millstone round our neck pulling us downwards, physically, mentally, emotionally and spiritually.

We grudgingly give time and effort and, so it seems, the problem always takes longer to solve than we imagine it will. That's because we are going about it in the wrong way.

If you treat the problem as part of the solution you will get on better. If you surround it with love the whole thing will be lighter in all respects. If you accept the problem is there for a very good reason you will treat it with respect. If you look for the message or lesson you will see it as an educating challenge.

All this will lighten your mood and you will find the insights, thus the solution will be easier to come by. Pouring out love will indeed dissolve the rough edges of your problem and make it far more manageable. Pouring out love will bring it into clearer focus, for you will be looking at it more as a friend than an enemy. Indeed you will have turned your enemy into a friend.

If you pour out love to everything and everyone in your life then your problems will surely be small and few.

The greatest power in the world is love.

How do you see problems? As obstacles or challenges? As delays or opportunities?

To what extent do you believe that unconditional love is the answer to problems?

17. Have no expectations of others and you will not be disappointed

How often have you shed tears because others didn't perform or say things you expected. If you build up these expectations there is a feeling of being let down and your world falling apart. God gave you and others free will and you have to allow them to use this in whatever way is right for them without judging.

You do not know their inner thoughts and feelings or what really motivates them. Accept others with love and without conditions attached. Your needs will be met but perhaps not in the way you expected. Allow the Universe to decide how to meet your needs. In your quiet moments send love to others and ask that whatever happens is for the highest good of all involved.

Remember others' actions don't just affect you. Be calm and loving and you will notice how everything works out. Expect nothing, demand nothing and you will receive everything you need.

How often have we felt let down when others didn't perform to a level we expected? It's a great way out of self blame if we can point to someone else and say that it was their fault, their inadequacy.

Too often we credit others with skills that they do not have, and have made no enquiry to find out what their abilities are. It's almost the same as being judgmental. We assume, imagine, convince ourselves our view is the correct one. But, as with making any judgment, you cannot be certain the view you hold is correct until you have examined and tested every detail.

Wouldn't it be better not to make any judgment at all? Withhold making an expectation and no matter what happens you should not be disappointed by the outcome. You may be surprised by it, but you won't be let down.

This may sound a very hit and miss approach to getting anything completed but there is a way you can help. That is to make contact with your Inner Being. Find out who you really are and where you are going. You Inner Being knows these things and will help you.

The more you seek your Self the more confident you will become in trusting and accepting the answers and feelings you will get. Your intuition will tell you about others in a non-judgmental way and you can base your everyday actions around what it tells you.

Instead of feeling disappointed when something goes wrong you will see the message or learn the lesson the event has brought. You will marvel and find warm feelings as you see that others will respond positively, perhaps also realising that there is a learning experience to be shared.

Having no expectations doesn't mean you are without drive or ambition. It means that you are a spiritual being walking your development path and recognise that everyone else is also doing that.

Expect nothing, demand nothing and you will receive everything you need.

Have you ever received help or guidance in an unexpected way?

When was the last time you felt you were let down?
What were the circumstances? What led to your conclusion?

Should a similar situation arise could you have a more loving, non-judgmental attitude towards it?

18. Abundance is a state of mind, not a state of finances

You can feel abundant without any riches and feel poor with all the money and grandeur in the world. Feeling abundant is an awareness that you have everything you need and this is accompanied by a feeling of joy.

Many who are rich are extremely unhappy and live in fear of losing what they have accumulated. This is due to their attachment to the physical world and loss of connection to their Higher Self. When one is concerned with accumulating possessions one is filled with fear of being without. One forms a desire to have power and develops a lack of concern for one's fellow beings.

When you consider how abundant you are do not just think about having money to pay bills and buy food. Consider the skills you've been given, the opportunities you have to serve others, the way in which the Universe provides for you. The list is endless. Filling your mind with thoughts of how abundant you are will ensure you remain that way. Share your abundance with others and as you give so will you receive.

Abundance is having enough of something to meet your needs. In the material world abundance is very often confused with wealth: that is, money. However, you can be extremely rich without being abundant.

As you go about your life in haste and hurry do you know what it is you are looking for? Have you set yourself goals? Are they achievable? Are they measurable? Will you want more when you finally get to the end?

What is it, exactly, you are seeking? A large house? A fast car? An enormous bank balance? These are all financial things and are purely physical. And even though they are physical they will cost you dearly in emotional and mental capacities, not to mention spiritual direction.

You could spend your life seeking items that do your spiritual progression no good at all. When you die you cannot take them with you on the next part of your journey, so why bother with the helter-skelter of a stressful life for no real reward? If you would only slow down and take some time to review your situation you would see how abundant you really are. With some changes in your thought pattern a realisation would dawn on you that what you think you need is not a true reflection of your real needs. A little change here and there in your life would make a vast difference overall and the end result would be a close match to what you really want.

Ask yourself what you want. Ask your Self. Your Inner Self, not your Ego. To do this properly you need to take the time and make the effort. Shut yourself away in a quiet spot for a short time and focus inwards. You will bypass Ego and meet your Inner Being. There you can converse and start to plan your future: a future that brings you abundance.

When you consider how abundant you are do not just think about having money to pay bills and buy food.

List everything for which you feel grateful. You may be surprised at how long your list becomes.

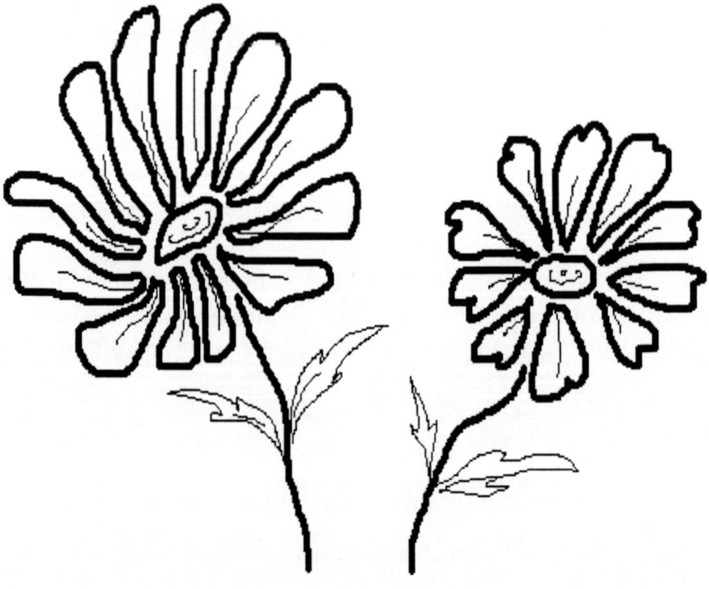

19. Pray with thanks and not with demands

So many people pray only when they are at rock bottom and in a crisis. Their prayers are filled with demands and requests which they hope God will instantly answer. They forget they have to play a part, and expect an instant change to take place. When nothing seems to change some of these people give up, saying there is no God or that God doesn't care about them.

These are not the best circumstances in which to pray. We say pray each day, indeed make every moment like a prayer. Be aware of all your thoughts and actions and ask if they have God-like qualities. When you take time off from your activities to pray by all means talk to God and ask for help. Go into the silence and listen for answers. You can't hear the help if you don't pay attention. Ask for what is going to assist your spiritual progress. Do not ask for lessons to be taken away but ask for guidance as to how to deal with them.

As you pray remember to include thanks for all that you have. This focuses and uplifts the mind reminding you of your blessings. This frame of mind will be the right one for handling whatever comes your way.

Prayer is often a last resort, carried out when all else has failed. Sometimes it is almost an act of desperation. At most other times it is carried out in a ritualistic manner with a form and structure that is human invention and theological practice.

People usually regard prayer as part of an act of worship. It's as if God demands it, or that prayer is the only way to communicate with the Divine. It needn't be like that for prayer is a channel to the Universe: it's how you "talk" to Creation, to All that is. It can be used at any time, in any situation.

Use prayer as you would engage another human: as a means of communication. In "normal" conversation you do not often make demands as part of your communication, so why make them when praying?

You get back what you give out, so if you keep making demands of the Universe, so, in some way there will be even greater demands made of you. There are so many things that have been provided for you by the Universe, yet you are blind to this. You take so many things for granted you scarcely acknowledge how they came to be.

Have you ever tried listing things you are given without your intervention, like sunshine, flowers, rain? Have you ever said "thank you" for air to breathe or water to drink?

Giving out appreciation and love has far greater rewards than always demanding. Have you never heard the maxim "I want never gets"? Yes, we would all like a lot of things, but do we need them? We carry on like children always asking for one more thing. You soon get tired of hearing children's demands, but then you do the same thing. Ever wonder where children learn from?

Look around you. List what you have, list what you really need. You are abundant but you don't realise it. Take time to consider your existence and when you have truly and honestly investigated it, realise that you do not have to make demands of Source because it is already doing more than well to provide you with what you need.

Go into the silence and listen for answers.

Do you only pray when you are in trouble?

Do you ask God / the Universe to provide what you think is the right solution or do you state your problem and trust that the right solution will appear?

20. Listen to the birds: they always have something to sing about

There are two messages here. First there is advice to take time to listen to nature. Be still and leave work so that you can tune into and blend with nature. Even a few minutes of stillness can become a meditation. Your attention is taken away from everyday problems and activities and is focussed on something peaceful. You will be refreshed and have a different attitude to what you have to do.

Secondly be aware of the trust that animals and birds have that all their needs will be met. Even in frosty weather in winter when the ground is hard and it is difficult for the birds to find enough food they still sing and give pleasure. The Universe provides for all. They live and enjoy each moment without fear for tomorrow or next week. Take a lesson from nature.

Be in the present no matter what your circumstances. Be grateful for what you have, be joyful and give thanks. This is trust. You have to know that your needs will be met and demonstrate that you really believe this. By spending time blending with nature you will find it easier to take on the positive qualities nature has to offer.

When you go for a walk in the park or some similar place or even when you sit in your urban garden you are always aware of the birdsong. If you look closer you will most often be able to see the bird that is singing. Often too, you will be able to identify the species of bird. If you are really good you will be able to identify the bird from its song!

But the point is that the birds are always singing and always it is a happy sound. It uplifts us. From morning until night the birds never stop, even although they have their lives to lead. They, like you, have to eat: they, like you, may have other mouths to feed also. They have to watch out for predators, they have to build their nests at appropriate times of the year.

They go about their business, their life, singing the joys of being alive. Theirs is a celebration of life and they will adapt and improvise without a second thought.

But what about us? When things go wrong or are delayed we grumble, grumble, grumble. More often than not it will be someone else's fault. Never is it ours. We allow ourselves to become disappointed and let our spirits fall. We let anger take over. We find it difficult to modify our plans. This is Ego driving us, and Ego is not interested in anything else but a selfish outcome.

If we were to allow our spiritual nature to come to the fore we would make better progress. We would see the big picture, we would not be rushing to judgment, we would not be dishing out blame to all and sundry. When delays hit us we would take that step back, looking for the message or the lesson to learn, adapting and moving on.

Always there is something to sing about, for the Universe is bountiful and takes care of us. The answer is always there. It's just that too often Ego hides it from us. The birds seem to know that all will be well and sing about it from the treetops. Isn't it time we learned that lesson too?

Take a lesson from nature.

What lessons does nature have to offer you?

Make time to commune with nature. . . a walk in the park, a seat by the river, tending your garden. Turn it into a meditation by allowing yourself to become absorbed by the natural sounds.

21. Judge others and you will be judging God

We are all part of the Creator and there is a spark of the Divine within all life. Souls incarnate into the physical to learn and grow, but sometimes whilst in the physical that Divine connection is forgotten. Do not criticise others for this. They are on their pathway back to God and although it will be different to yours, the journeys will terminate in the same place.

Know that all life is connected and look beyond what is visible to the physical eyes. Love others without judging, for if you judge and criticise you are in fact judging yourself and God. All is one. Accept this and you will find it easy to practise unconditional love.

Do not be harsh on yourself but continually monitor your own thoughts and actions. A notebook or diary with daily entries will assist your progress. Note down each day what occurred, how you reacted, how you felt. Ask yourself what lesson was being presented and the insights gained. Go to sleep in peace knowing that you are willing to learn and that your Ego is taking a back seat as the God within shines forth.

God is many things to many people. It has always been this way, since the dawn of civilisation. It will probably go on in this manner until everyone comes to the same view.

Usually we are referring to the Divine when we use the word "God". It matters not whether the belief is in an unseen all-powerful omnipresent being or in a concept. What is true is that, since we are part of God's creation, we all contain a spark of the Divine within us.

We are all manifestations of God, as is everything around us in the world we inhabit. We are creations of God, all different, but all nonetheless wonderful.

So when we as individuals express ourselves we are in effect making a comment on creation. When we sit in judgement we pour out our scorn and disappointment, usually without knowing the full details. We give out negativity. We have made a judgement on what God has created!

Are we better than God? There is no need for me to answer that question.

If you don't like something or someone, walk away. If you feel you need to do something about it then choose your words carefully and treat the situation with love and respect.

God has created all these wonders so that we might learn and develop. Everything is here for a purpose so look for it. Educate yourself. Prosper. Develop. But please, do not criticise or judge for that will do no one any good.

We all contain a spark of the Divine within us.

Can you see any positive qualities in someone you find it difficult to get on with?

Have you written your journal entry for today?

What happened to you during the course of the day?

How did you react?

What were your thoughts?

Was there a message for you or a lesson to learn?

22. A rich harvest is the reward for much effort

We in the Higher Realms are here to assist and guide you when you invite us to draw close. Whenever you ask for help it will be given. The Universe provides for everyone's needs but this doesn't mean that no effort is required on the part of individuals: you have to play your part. We do not wave a magic wand as this would not provide you with any lessons or growth. The spiritual path is not an easy option. Obstacles come up which have to be negotiated.

Do not stray from your pathway and do not give up. Every success will assist further progress. Your efforts will produce joy, peace and satisfaction. You have been given freedom of choice. Do not fall for the easy option as it may hold you back. Practise unconditional love, not just for others, but for circumstances you have to deal with. Look for spiritual answers and ask for strength to put them into practice.

The easy pathway requires little effort but the harvest is poor and the future tough. The spiritual pathway requires action and effort, but the good harvest will provide nourishment for the future.

The rain and sunshine provide the right environment for the growth of plants for food but these crops require much attention in order to flourish and provide a bountiful harvest. The Universe doesn't just take care of our harvests but provides for everything we need on all levels.

It is easy to blame other people and circumstances when things do not work out as we'd like. By taking responsibility, and understanding that we have the ability to create our reality, we can find abundance and joy.

By taking time daily to tune into the Higher Realms and ask for guidance to live by the Laws of the Universe we can be in harmony with all life. Effort is required daily to put these Universal Laws into practice and if we do so we will have a rich harvest every day. It takes time and effort to ensure you are sharing your gifts with others and not stockpiling for yourself. Say thanks every day for whatever you have received, share what you have with others and trust that your harvest will always be rich enough to meet your needs.

At the beginning of each year the farmers prepare their fields before planting the seeds that will eventually produce foodstuffs. From grains to vegetables the process is the same. The farmers toil hard in the fields, and, with favourable weather conditions, they reap the crop.

So too with your life. You have to prepare for what you want to achieve. You have to work hard to ensure your goals are being met and at the end you are rewarded with success. Just as the weather can be unpredictable for the farmers, you will also have to face up to challenges of items beyond your control, but you should have planned for variations in your preparations, just in case.

Even in "bad" years the farmers still produce food. You should be able to produce results too, even when the going gets tough. It is when conditions are not favourable that your resolve and creativity should be at their height. You need to have that determination to win through. Commitment is the key to success. If you are going to be knocked from the path at the first stumbling block then it is hardly worth starting at all.

Like an enemy, bad times occur to tell you something about yourself. There is a message for you and you should always seek it out. Once you have discovered the message you can continue your quest a stronger, more knowledgeable person. If you stick with the task you will find bad times, like the wind, soon blow over and the calm returns.

Do not be put off from achieving what you set out to do. There is joy in achieving a goal, but there is much joy in achieving a goal when bad times have intervened. Ironically it is the bad times that tell us if we are committed or not. If we are, we march on to a great reward.

Say thanks every day for whatever you have received.

List five things for which you were thankful today.

How can you deal with obstacles which distract you from your spiritual development?

What lessons / messages did you pick up from your last "bad" time?

23. If you feel lonely look to the Angels for company

Angels are a group of beings dedicated to assisting humanity. Angels are always close by and watching over you even although you may not be aware of their presence. They desire to be of service but must be invited to assist as they will not interfere with your free will. Some people are able to see them or sense their presence. However, this is not necessary in order to work with the Angels.

Whenever you feel alone or let down by others just call on the Angels for company by sitting quietly and making your needs known: do not ask for anything that is unloving or selfish. The Angels can bring you many different qualities according to your needs. Know your needs, send out a thought to the Angels and know they will respond.

There are Angels to assist with all aspects of your life: there are Angels of Healing, Angels of Light, Angels of Hope, Angels of Trust to name but a few. They bring a variety of qualities such as love, forgiveness, and creativity. Ask and you will receive. With each breath fill your whole being with the qualities you would like.

Remember that even when you are alone you can share these qualities with others. Send out love and healing and you will make the connection at a higher level. If you cannot see the Angels this doesn't matter. Imagine what you think they look like, trust they are all around you and thank them for their presence and upliftment.

By calling on the Angels you will be lifting up your mind to the realms of love, and, as you will be surrounded by them, you will not be alone.

Trust that the Angels can bring about beneficial outcomes, take time each day to invite the Angels to protect and guide you, and take note of the difference this makes to your life.

You won't find better company than a Company of Angels around you protecting you with love.

Everyone, without exception, has a Guardian Angel watching over them at all times. Often there will be other Angels and Beings of Light in attendance also. The Angels, if we may use that word as a collective term for those beings of light, are there for you to consult on any matter at any time. Angels will not interfere with your free will but they are aware of your soul's purpose. They can guide you, they can advise you, but they will never decide for you. Whatever you do will be down to you, for each person creates their own reality.

Mostly people only turn to the Angels when things are going wrong or when they have reached a crisis point in their life. It's almost the last resort to reach out to the Angels, a final act of desperation. Of course the Angels will respond, and, in some cases, "miracles" seem to happen.

It needn't get to the desperation point. The Angels are in constant attention. They are always available for consultation. Sadly, we seem to forget this when life seems so good and many never give the Angels a second thought.

Everyone can make contact with their Angels on a daily basis. Chat to them, confide in them, and tell them how you feel. Listen to what they have to say. There is much that can be learned by doing this.

When you go into the quiet to consult your Higher Self, ask the Angels to get involved too. You may be amazed at what can happen.

Angels are there for you to consult on any matter at any time.

Can you list some ideas for involving Angels in your day to day activities?

Did you consult your Guardian Angel today?

24. A few minutes quiet each day can save hours of disquiet

You know how true this is from your own experiences. You know how much you have suffered when you barge on facing difficulties without taking time to stop and be still. When these problems occur they seem to snowball with one difficulty leading to subsequent issues. You tumble from one issue to another, taking all the fear and resentment from each one to the next without taking time to recharge your batteries.

You know the benefits of quiet periods from a physical and emotional point of view. It stills the body and mind. You can see more clearly afterwards and the problem doesn't seem so bad. Very often there isn't a problem at all. By being still and distanced from the situation you realise it is not as important as it first appeared.

You can call on our presence and healing, and we are always pleased when you do this rather than see you struggle alone. In these quiet moments you have learned to send out love to situations and you have seen the benefits. You have learned that everything happens in the right way, at the right time and that all is love.

It isn't easy, when faced with problems, to be disciplined enough to take time away from them but you know it is the wise thing to do and the benefits are enormous. This is a precious ability to have but not everyone realises this or is willing to give it a go. It is something that everyone has to do for themselves. Spend your energy wisely. Create harmony with your thoughts instead of unhappiness with your words and actions.

Quiet. We all know the dictionary explanation, but do we ever achieve it? No! Can we ever achieve it? Who knows? Always, particularly in the cities, there is noise, there is bustle. We have become used to much of this background noise, and mostly it doesn't bother us. But that's not what we are talking about here. The quiet referred to here means to take time away from everyday activities. To find a place where we can be undisturbed by others, by phones and suchlike. A place where we can sit, in solitude if wished, and contemplate on matters.

Quiet. The place where we discover ourselves. The place where we get in touch with our Higher Self, our Inner Being. The place where Ego does not enter. In the quiet you can have time to think about who you are, what your purpose is, where you are going. In the quiet you can plan your journey in life, your journey through life. Without Ego getting in the way you can make decisions based on love and understanding. In the quiet you will find out how you really feel and will act accordingly. There is no Ego telling you what to think, do and say.

The disquiet of worry and anger will be dispersed by your Inner Being and its wisdom. Your Inner Being will not give you wrong answers. Your Inner Being will always act in your best interests. Your conscience will be clear because you will have no doubts about your actions.

Without the quiet, Ego takes over and can get you into difficulties. You will act without thinking. You may resort to anger and rage. Grudges may develop. All these are negative reactions and will attract only negative responses. The wisdom of quiet does not go there. Quiet will show you the positive in all situations and allow you to build on it. Positive reactions attract positive responses.

Look for the quiet and learn much.

Create harmony with your thoughts

Why not take a few moments quiet now and see for yourself the difference it can make.

Do you monitor and control your thoughts or do they run riot, creating bad situations for you?

What actions could you take to bring harmony to your reality?

25. Don't just listen to others: listen to yourself as well

It's easier to listen to others than to listen to yourself. You can enjoy listening to their stories, providing an ear for their sorrows and problems, but you can have two deaf ears when it comes to listening to yourself. This is why it's important to make time for this. You have to set aside time, and also be continually aware of when you should be listening to yourself.

Others come along, start talking and you listen. It's not quite so simple with yourself. You have to be still or you miss that calm, small voice within or that inner feeling that can guide you and tell you so much. It's easier to bash on allowing that conscious mind to dictate what to do or what to say. It analyses things like a computer and an answer comes up just as it does on a calculator or on a computer screen.

You can carry on doing several things at a time whilst this analytical mind provides you with your next course of action. It's not always in your best interests but it's an easy quick option especially when time is at a premium.

It is helpful to learn the word 'stop'. Stop the analytical thoughts rushing around and get in touch with yourself. That can mean sitting down quietly, perhaps concentrating on a meditative symbol, and allowing the mind to still so that your Higher Self gets a word in edgeways. You wouldn't keep barging in when someone is trying to tell you their problem. You listen and take in what's said, but your Higher Self doesn't always get this chance to speak.

You can get more done, make more progress, make the right decisions if you listen to your Spiritual Self. It may not be an easy option but it will be the right one.

Listening to yourself isn't just about sitting in a meditative posture in a silent room. It's about constantly being in touch with you inner feelings. It's easy to block out feelings, and these are so important. Learn to stop, and acknowledge these gut feelings. They will tell you so much and will rarely be wrong.

Feelings are a communication and should be acknowledged. Just take a moment many times a day and ask yourself how you are feeling. Make it a habit and you will notice the difference.

Others can be very quick to offer you advice and opinion, even when it's not wanted. Others can be very keen for you to hear what they have to say, especially if they are on an Ego trip or want to dominate your life in some way.

There will never be a shortage of others telling you what is best for you. How do they know what's best for you? The short answer is they don't. What they are telling you is not necessarily in your best interests, but, it is certainly in theirs. Hopefully when others give you advice and opinions you will consider carefully what they have to say.

Even if you have asked for their advice it is always in your best interests to consider what has been offered, for you don't want to give away your free will and blithely follow the advice offered.

So, in considering what has been said do you ever ask your own Higher Self for an opinion? Do you ever listen to what your Inner Being has to say?

Your Inner Being is not driven by Ego. In fact you have bypassed Ego to talk to your Inner Being. Therefore pride and standing will also have been bypassed, and what you will get is an honest answer to your enquiries. From the heart of your Being you will get answers, opinions, options. You will get truth, and always the answer will be for the benefit of everyone involved in the situation.

There will be no selfish outcomes, no taking a stand on something because Ego demanded it. Just good, honest, down-to-earth possibilities. It will then be for you to make the decision because your free will remains under your control. What better outcome could you ask for?

Others' advice is important, but in matters that affect you, your Inner Being is more important and you should listen to yourself before you make any decisions.

It is helpful to learn the word 'stop'.

When did you last stop and listen to your Higher Self?

Do you allocate time at the end of the day to go into the quiet and just listen for guidance from the Universe?

26. Ask for guidance but remember to listen for answers

We would never interfere with the free will you have been given and therefore we would not offer help unless you ask for this. We will not forsake you if you request our presence and assistance. Never feel you are alone. When you feel you do not have the answers to problems it usually means you are fighting back at a physical level.

This is unlikely to provide a permanent solution as problems will reappear until you have dealt with them spiritually. When you are troubled and stressed it is more difficult to sit quietly, relax, and go within for guidance. Step back from the problem. Spend a few minutes settling yourself and ask for guidance.

You may find it helpful to clarify your problem by writing it down. Ask us to connect with you and we will link in with love. We cannot solve problems but we can assist by reminding you of how to adopt a spiritual approach. However, assistance will be inadequate unless those who need help are prepared to play their part.

After stating your problems and asking for guidance as to how to cope, remain still in body and mind. If the mind is active and filled with anxious thoughts you are blocking out the possibility of guidance.

A still mind is a screen for answers to be projected onto, but a cluttered mind has no space for enlightenment. It can be helpful to keep a pen and paper handy to write down any ideas at the end of the quiet time.

Do your best to bring this calmness back with you as you go about whatever tasks you have to do. Your Higher Self will keep working with you and you will find you continue to receive guidance and direction in many different ways.

Ideas may come to you or you may find that you are directed to certain people or books for enlightenment. By maintaining a loving mind you will be open to direction and help.

Know that nothing occurs by chance and that answers may crop up in the most unlikely places. Look and listen for guidance, not just in quiet moments, but in everything you do.

When you are unsure of what to do, having considered what you believe to be all the options, you tend to send out a prayer for assistance. Your Ego has somehow failed you and you are at a loss. You then, almost in desperation, turn to your spiritual side, hoping against hope that it can provide an answer. In these sorts of circumstances you never really hear the answer for you are overtaken by fears and other emotions.

What we say to you is consider making your last hope your first hope, and actively listen for what is suggested. Go inwards and pose the question, and you may be surprised at the answers that come out of the quiet.

Ego will make demands, Ego will take control and make your decisions for you. How are you to know that what your Ego says is in your best interests or indeed everyone's best interests?

Your Higher Self will make suggestions, offer considerations, guidance, explanation, but it will not make demands. Your Higher Self is your true self and will offer what is best for you on your spiritual journey. Always the Law of Free Will is applied and you have the choice.

This is the advantage of listening to guidance: you make the choice. No more blindly following the Ego that cares only for itself.

Take time each day to set aside for quiet, inward contemplation. Ask whatever you want, but remember to listen to what is coming back to you. Listen, ponder, then use your free will to make the best decision. Make the decision that feels best to you. If you are inwardly happy then that is what is best in the circumstances.

The key to moving forward is to listen. How else are you going to hear the answer? Listening is a skill you can develop, and the best way to do so is to make contact with your Higher Self. Whatever answer you run with will always be the right one for you, and you can take confidence from this.

You will be better able to listen to others and see bigger pictures. You will understand more and act with greater wisdom. Wouldn't that be wonderful?

Look and listen for guidance in everything you do.

Before you begin your next quiet time write down a list of all those issues that are troubling you. Then, when you enter the quiet, ask for guidance on them, remembering to clear your mind of clutter and wayward thoughts. Have pen and paper handy so that you can record any answers that may be given.

Remember you can receive answers at unexpected times and not just during your quiet moments, so having a notebook handy at all times will help you to record them.

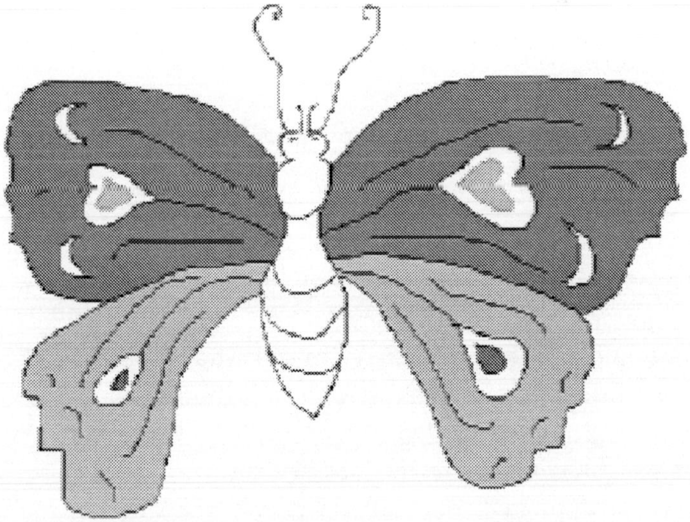

27. Knowledge comes from outside, Wisdom from inside.

Children begin acquiring knowledge from an early age. They are given information from many sources, including parents and teachers. This is often clouded with other people's opinions and ideas.

Even when adulthood is reached it can be hard to shake off knowledge that has been stored up. It can be difficult to know what is worth retaining and what is not useful.

When we go within to connect with our Higher Self we receive wisdom which will be exactly right for us at that moment of time. Wisdom enables us to live our lives, make decisions in an unselfish way which benefits everyone. Being wise isn't about being more intelligent than anyone else or about having vast amounts of knowledge in the brain. Everyone has the ability to be wise. It takes time and effort, just like acquiring knowledge but it will come from an inner knowing and not an external source.

Wisdom is what feels right to you: you know it makes sense. Wisdom is an inner knowing which cannot be learned from an external source. When filled with challenges look within for the wisdom to guide you.

Knowledge is what you acquire in your everyday activities. It is what you learn about yourself and your world. It is an understanding of how things work or why things should be so. However, knowledge is not necessarily constant in its accuracy, as different conclusions may be drawn from the same set of data or circumstances.

Attitudes and beliefs can interfere with knowledge. Similarly Ego can get in the way, and you may not be given the whole story or all the facts. Knowledge is seen by some as power, and by withholding information it can seem like they control who is to know what. It is also said that a little knowledge is a dangerous thing meaning that you cannot make any judgments or reach any conclusion until you are certain you know all the facts.

Wisdom, on the other hand, is knowing how to apply the knowledge gained. Wisdom is that still voice of calm within you. In some respects wisdom can be said to be like your gut feeling, that intuitive reaction that happens when a situation arises. How often do you listen? How often do you accept what it has to say? How often do you consult it? How often do you wish you had listened to it and gone along with it?

Wisdom is the advice of your Higher Self. As we have already said, your Higher Self will always take care of you. Your Higher Self will not allow its advice to hurt or harm you. You should listen to it more. You should consult it more often. Take time, make time each day to ask your Higher Self about what you are doing and where, in spiritual terms, you are going. It has no delusions, no power craze: therefore it will tell you truly and honestly. There is no good in blaming all else for your situation: it is the reality you created for yourself. However, you have a very good friend in your Higher Self, so why not get to know it even better?

Knowledge is learning, wisdom is knowing.

Wisdom is knowing how to apply the knowledge gained.

How do you know when something is right for you?

Where does that wisdom come from?

When was the last time you listened to your inner voice of wisdom?

28. The higher you rise above your problems the smaller they appear.

As you walk up a mountain the individual landmarks seem to become smaller and smaller. At the same time you get a bird's eye view with more of the landscape coming into your vision. It is a similar experience going up in an aeroplane. As you rise higher individual buildings become insignificant and you gain an overall impression of the land beneath you.

When you become focussed on a particular problem it is easy to view it with tunnel vision. It alone fills your mind, and it is difficult to see what options are available. The problem appears huge and the solutions seem to be hidden from sight.

Find a peaceful place and allow time to set aside problems. With a clear mind you can allow your consciousness to rise above the everyday turmoil. As your mind is allowed to rise upwards you can take in light instead of being surrounded by the darkness of your difficulties. Your mind can bring everything into perspective. It becomes possible, due to this wider view, to understand how events in life are linked and what teachings they can bring. They will no longer seem huge and insurmountable.

Your physical view may be limited but at a spiritual level everything is meaningful and connected.

When you are deeply engrossed in something the tiniest detail appears huge, so you believe the whole thing must be unbelievably large. When you scrutinise in such a detailed manner you cannot see the boundaries or edges. Because you cannot see the edges you get caught up in a maze, believing that there is no end.

Problems are like this. Our inclination is to get to the heart or root of the problem believing that that is where we will find the solution. In the majority of cases this approach only damages our perspective, and everything gets magnified as already described. We get lost in the problem and we become despondent. The problem gets to us and we become miserable. It is when reaching into the problem doesn't bring a solution that we should stop and look outside the situation. We should stand back from it and thus make ourselves bigger than the problem, not the other way round.

You have seen pictures of the planet taken from space. How small, beautiful and tranquil it looks. Yet we all have a different perception from the surface. How big, unfriendly and frightening it can be.

Take the cosmic view and you will see much more. Do you really need to worry about the tiniest detail? You probably do not look at every small detail of everything you come into contact with, so why do it with problems?

Step back. See the big picture. See where the problem lies in the scale of things, then deal with it at a more appropriate level. It is said that "fools rush in where wise men fear to tread", so when problems arise, act like a wise man, and take time to see the whole picture. Rise above it and see it for what it is.

Your physical view may be limited but at a spiritual level everything is meaningful and connected.

Do you have a situation you are unsure how to resolve? Go into the quiet and raise up your consciousness. Visualise yourself looking down on the problem: see where it fits in. Is it really as bad as when you were immersed in it at a physical level?

29. Lighten your load: fill yourself with light.

When we become depressed or anxious our whole body is affected. It has been said that it can seem like carrying a weight on the shoulders. We slow down as if we are carrying a burden which hinders our movement. The mind cannot stop churning over problems which seem to have no end and no solution. Everything becomes difficult and even simple tasks can seem unbearable.

A load on the mind creates a load on the body. All this creates numerous health problems. It is therefore beneficial to lighten the load on the mind. In difficult times it can be easy to miss out on quiet times for meditation, but this is the time when the benefits can truly be seen.

It is an opportunity to put trust in the Universe and link up to the Beings of Light who can assist you. Still the mind and ask for light and love to fill your whole being. Send light and love to whatever your difficulty might be and ask for the right outcome for all involved.

As you return from this period of stillness allow yourself to bring back the qualities which will enable you to handle whatever you are faced with. Know that all things work out for the best if you allow the Universe to take care of everything.

Keep a clear mind filled with light, look after your body as well, and you will move forward with a positive attitude.

There are times when you believe you are carrying all the troubles of the world on your shoulders. This is when life for you is not running smoothly. It is strange that when life is not good we perceive the load to be heavy. We perceive all that is not good to be weighing us down. It is the weight we attach to those somewhat immeasurable things that stops us from making progress. Perhaps it's not so strange that light is both the opposite of heavy and dark.

In our times of trouble we should be looking at the bigger picture, as explained elsewhere. [The higher you rise above your problems…] Perhaps we are getting too embroiled in our misery to look outside it.

Every burden brings with it an opportunity for self discovery. It is not a random happening, with you as an unfortunate victim. Some see it like this and walk slowly through the darkness, stumbling from one crisis to the next.

However, if you look for the message behind the burden you will literally see the light. Learn the lesson and flood yourself with light. Life will become simpler and your progress will be quicker. Better to let the light in than to stumble in the dark. The light, if you let it, will penetrate all your dark recesses. Your heavy load will become more manageable, and, with constant revision of your situation, you will get to that point of spontaneous joy. When you do, you will know that you have indeed filled yourself with light. Lighten up and be a beacon for others.

A load on the mind creates a burden on the body.

How does your physical body feel when you have worries on your mind? Do you suffer headaches, digestive problems, poor concentration, etc?

Isn't it time to link up to the realms of light and trust the Universe to take care of issues for you?

What issues are weighing you down? Are there any you carry around with you just for the sake of it?

Which ones could you unload?
(a) Now
(b) With a little work

30. Life doesn't have to be complicated unless you choose it to be: simplicity brings peace.

When difficult situations arise it is easy to become anxious and frustrated. It can become hard to think clearly and see a way out. The more stressed you become the more the problem becomes magnified and complicated. It is easy to go round in circles without making any progress. Fear is a major cause of stress, and if a different outlook is achieved difficulties can be resolved.

It is important to realise we create our thoughts and our reality. When we understand this we gain control of our lives which become simpler and more peaceful.

View each event as an experience which provides growth. Be grateful for it, and instead of being filled with fear, send out love and ask your Higher Self to guide you through it. Know that there is a purpose in everything. Be positive and trusting, knowing that you are being taken care of. If you believe life to be complicated then that is what it will be. Be thankful for all the good things you have been given. Believe that all is as it is meant to be, and you will experience peace of mind at all times.

Life does seem so complex for many of you, but that is because you have made it that way. Your thoughts are Ego driven and your reality is not the one you would have chosen had you gone inwards first of all. Ego has led you into all sorts of relationships with all sorts of results and consequences.

You have a saying "keep it simple" and this is good advice, for you make things easier when you simplify them.

Examine your relationships. Who are they with? What do you get from them? Do they bring you benefit? Can you change what is wrong? Can you simplify?

Try to keep Ego out of your analysis, for it was Ego that created your current reality. Step back from it, and look with unbiased eyes. If you are happy with what you find then well done. If you are not then you must consider making changes.

Your modern world lives at a fast pace, almost on the edge. This is especially so in the larger cities. When you visit a small village you can see the difference. It is so much quieter, and people seem happier.

Can you slow down the pace at which you perform? Only you will know the answer. As we have said, if you feel your life is too complex examine it for what is going on. Identify the parts you want to change, then do it with commitment.

You make things easier when you simplify them.

What are the complex parts of your life?

How can you simplify them?

What skills / tools / attitudes would you need?

31. Don't just cleanse the body, cleanse the mind as well. Freshen up with pure thoughts.

It is wise to pay attention to your body, taking adequate exercise and consuming a healthy, balanced diet. Good health depends on how you treat your body. If you neglect your body this can lead to being lethargic and even depressed.

The mind and body are connected so it is important to pay attention to both. If the mind is filled with worry the stress on the systems of the body can be enormous.

When you rise each morning pay attention to your thoughts. As well as taking care to cleanse your body, fill your mind with positive thoughts and this will get your day off to a good start. Greet the day with thanks, and have a positive state of mind knowing that whatever circumstances you have to face you will cope well. Keep examining your thoughts regularly throughout the day to ensure you are calm and peaceful.

At the end of the day again give thanks, and fill your mind with love and gratitude for the day that is now ending. By caring for your body and mind you will experience balance and good health which will be an example for others to follow.

As you take a shower you may think that you are washing away the dust of the day. Cleansing the skin in hot soapy water gives an uplifting feeling. So too does a soak in a hot bath where perhaps you can relax in the warmth. But do you ever clear away the debris from your mind? Inside your head you have more knowledge and facts stored away than you can ever use. Sometimes you find it difficult to recall what is needed because everything is cluttered.

Also inside your head you are carrying other people's thoughts and beliefs. Over the years you have been conditioned by other influences. If you are happy with this situation then all is well. If you are not then isn't it time to have a clearout?

Is it time for you to examine who you are and why you are here? Do you ever wonder why you think the way you do? Would it surprise you to know that everything you are and do, and everything that happens to you is created by you?

Your thoughts are your reality. If it doesn't exist in your mind then it doesn't exist anywhere. Is your reality what you want it to be? Are you happy with what you do? Only you can change your reality. No one else can. They might influence you, but only you can make the change, if you want to.

Next time you are soaking in the bath why not take some time to cleanse your mind at the same time. Perhaps you will emerge feeling great inside and out.

Over the years you have been conditioned by other influences.

What beliefs do you hold?

Where did they come from?

Do you need to change or discard any of these?

32. Let the soul feed the mind, and the mind feed the body.

If the mind is allowed to run riot with many unpleasant and negative thoughts this affects the physical body. Imbalance is created within the body as it struggles to cope with the stress created. To achieve health and balance a clear mind is necessary. As you sit in a meditative state the clear mind can reflect the impressions your soul wishes to make. Ask your soul to give guidance so that you can follow your spiritual path. A cloudy mind inhibits a clear reflection and no guidance can be impressed on it. A mind filled with pure thoughts, positive affirmations and love will allow the body to maintain its equilibrium. The soul knows what is right for you, and you won't go wrong if you take time to tune in regularly. How can you know your soul's purpose if you don't listen? By tuning into the higher frequency you gain the ability to control your mind and therefore your thinking. A healthy mind produces a healthy body.

Balance is achieved when body, mind and spirit work in harmony. Connect with your soul, and the energy received will feed your mind and, in turn, your body. Refuel each day to maintain balance and health.

Everyone has a Soul purpose, a reason for being here. We all have a spiritual job to perform. This is why we incarnated. Very often the experience of being in a relatively low vibratory body seems to have the effect of making us forget what that purpose is, and we drift along, living a life that is often adequate, but not fulfilling. For many this is life: there is nothing else, for they have completely lost their spiritual connection. For some, and the number is growing, the connection is re-established, and the soul's purpose can begin to be achieved. When we know who we are and what our purpose is we can change from a mundane sort of existence to a more meaningful one.

In this state of being we connect easily and frequently with our Soul, and are reminded of what it is we are hoping to achieve. The Soul will not misdirect, but neither will it insist. It will offer advice, suggest an outcome. It is up to each of us to make the final decision as to whether or not we do something. So when the Soul has something to say it plants seeds of ideas into the mind. In the mind these seeds will grow to form into ideas, beliefs, etc. From thoughts to actions is the acceptance by the body of these Soul-inspired notions. Now it is reality. The process means that your Soul's purpose can be fulfilled. By accepting its notions and processing them through ideas and thoughts into the reality (your reality) of action you are demonstrating to everyone who you really are and are making progress on the journey you laid out before you were born. The outgoings of the Soul are no Egotistical rant: they are the expression of who you are and where you are going.

Of course you have the choice. You can go with them and discover enlightenment or you can ignore them, and completely miss the point. Which way will be your choice?

Refuel each day to maintain balance and health.

What fuel do you need to take in?

Where will it come from?

Do you have the commitment to see this through?

33. One candle can light many others. Share your light with those who need it.

A candle once lit can not only light many others but those it lights can themselves light numerous others. Think how much light can be produced when one candle shares its light.

When you connect with your spiritual self you are allowing love and light to flow into your being. Open your heart centre and allow this light to flow from you to where it is needed. It may be to friends, family, relationships, other forms of life on the planet and to countries which need your assistance. Fill yourself with light each day, and others will notice and benefit from it. Many people are spending their life surrounded by darkness. Allow your aura to touch them, and ask that they may receive light from you if this is in their best interests.

Those who benefit from your light can, in turn, assist others. The effect can be enormous just like the example of the candles. Keep your light switched on, and the effect will be beneficial to many, most of whom you may never even meet.

One candle in the darkness may not sound much, but it certainly takes the edge off it. It can be seen from a great distance too. One little flame in all that darkness. All it has taken has been one spark to light it, and it brings so much comfort.

Like the words say, that candle can then be used to light countless others. If this were to happen the darkness would virtually disappear. When someone has a good idea it is often depicted as a light being switched on over their heads. It is the same when you reach for the Higher Vibrations: you fill yourself with light. As you walk your spiritual path that light will shine outwards for all to see.

By your example you can inspire others to grow in light too. Where there is darkness your light will allow you to penetrate and show the way. We say "your" light because it emerges from you, but in reality it is the one light and is for all. Therefore the light within you is for sharing, for giving out. It is not for you to accumulate or hide.

Whatever light is within you is for giving out to relieve the darkness. It is for you to help others find their way, for once they have seen the light they can start to generate it themselves. Every one and every thing has the potential, and each one who has it should be realising the potential to make it happen. That way the whole planet evolves and ascension to the next level happens.

You can inspire others to grow in light too.

Who could benefit from your light right now?

From the darkness came the light,
A day of glory to follow the night.
Let your light shine to show the way,
Can you make this world a better place today?

34. Every act is a choice: you always have an option.

How often have you heard people say that they had no choice as to how they acted or as to what they said? It can sound as though they were forced into a certain set of circumstances due to the part played by another person. This is apportioning blame instead of accepting responsibility. Every act is a choice, and even when one refuses to act or to make changes this is still a decision, and hence a choice has been made.

Take care to make choices based on love and not to get your own back on someone. Understand the implications of your actions and realise that for every action there is a reaction. Act in such a way that you will have no regrets in the future. Do your best to ensure you use your power positively, and do not sit back refusing to make changes. Getting into a rut does not enable you to develop and move forward. Have courage to make choices, but take time to weigh up the consequences. There are always choices to be made but you can't progress unless you make decisions and act on them. Do not sit back and let others make choices for you. Make your own, but do so lovingly.

It has been stated many, many times that everybody, each one of you, has the gift of free will. Through this gift you are able to do whatever you want. It is a gift from Source and shouldn't be given away, for to do so means you are giving away your very being. If you do not use your free will you may have to submit to someone else's, and that is not really such a good idea, for you will end up doing things, not because you want to, but because you have to.

Keeping hold of your free will means you are in control of your being and your reality. You decide what happens. You decide what you want to do. It is your responsibility to express your free will, for it determines who you are and where you are going. Every act you perform will have been decided upon by you. Always there is a choice. To do or not to do is the simplest choice, but there will be occasions when the choice is greater than this.

How will you make the choice? Will you let Ego make it or will you consult your Higher Self? There is a difference between making a choice and making the right choice: right, that is, for you. The best choices are made with love and understanding: the worst are made in haste and anger.

Remember, what you give out you get back, so just ask what you'd like to receive in return before you opt for a particular course of action. Will it bring you what you need?

You don't have to act in a hurry, for that will cause you to miss considerations. Better late in some respects for at least you have had time to have looked at your options in more detail. Consult your Inner Self, act in love, and choose, knowing that you have opted to act in everyone's best interests.

Every act is a choice: for every action there is a reaction.

What factors influence your choice making?

Do you always consider the reaction for yourself and others?

Are you always involved in the decision making on issues that affect you?

35. Be guided by your Higher Self, not your Ego

If you wish to follow your spiritual pathway and be of service to humanity you have to be able to control the Ego and link up with your Higher Self. The Ego will always try to direct to ensure its needs are met. Often this will be in conflict with your Higher Self which knows what is best for you. The Ego can be selfish and materialistic, but your Higher Self is there to guide you spiritually towards the goal you set yourself before this incarnation. Your Higher Self operates on a love vibration and will point you on the right pathway to enable you to display your spiritual qualities.

You may not always understand why you are being directed along a particular pathway, but your Higher Self has to be trusted.

If you are constantly focussed on what your Ego is telling you, you are blocking out guidance from your Higher Self. It is important to be silent, still the mind and ask your Higher Self to communicate. This may come as ideas, words, pictures or symbols. You may not receive an instant answer but may find that days or even weeks later you are directed to a particular source of information which is just what you need.

In a sense there can be conflict within you. You can be stretched in different directions and still have an affinity with each. How do you decide? You often talk of heart ruling head or vice versa. You use the expression about the left hand not knowing what the right one is doing. It all points to a body in conflict, to a body that has actually lost direction.

How do you solve this problem? Do you just make a snap decision or go with the loudest shout? Really the first question ought to be "Who am I?" followed by "Why am I here?". When you can answer these questions you can then ask, "Which direction takes me to where I want to be that is in keeping with my aims and objectives?".

In short you need to communicate with your Inner Being or Higher Self. Here is your connection to the Universe, and the answers to the first two questions. How often do you take time, make time, to do this? Your Higher Self will guide you, but not dominate you. Your Higher Self will allow you to decide. Your Higher Self will paint the bigger picture for you to consider.

Ego on the other hand is that part of you that makes demands without looking at outcomes. Ego will direct you to a decision that may have serious consequences. Ego will not try to protect you. Ego does as Ego wants. Ego bursts forth upon you uncalled.

This is not so with your Higher Self as it waits patiently to be consulted. Yes, sometimes Higher Self tries to guide you unasked. This is what we call "gut feeling" or "intuition". Make time each day just to go into the quiet, and consult your Higher Self. You will be amazed at what awaits you. As you often say "you never knew you had it in you!" Believe me you have, and you should use it more frequently. Take time to do this, it will be well spent.

Who am I?
Why am I here?

If you are serious about following your spiritual pathway pose these questions to your Higher Self in your next meditation.

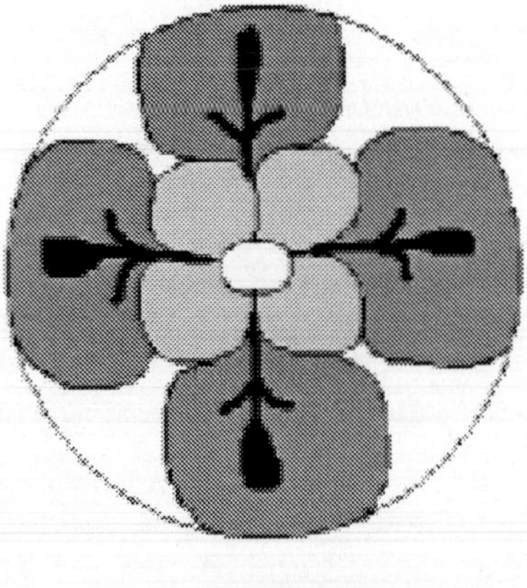

36. Intentions are important. What are your intentions for today?

Nothing can be achieved if you do not have the intention of doing it. If you state what you intend, the Universe will listen and assist you. There is no point in drifting along with no goals in mind. This wastes time, with nothing positive achieved. It is demoralising and no progress is made.

Ask for assistance, and you will receive help. You have free will so no help will be given unless you request it. Stating your intention invokes assistance from the Higher Realms so long as what you intend is for the highest good of all concerned. It is helpful to write down your intentions to remind yourself of them.

At the start of each day spend a few moments considering your intentions for the day. This will put you in the right frame of mind, and you are less likely to waste your day on the wrong activities.

Intention isn't just about activities. It's about emotions and feelings as well. Start your day with the intention of maintaining positive feelings and emotions, and the desire to be open to giving and receiving love.

Have the intention to meet all situations with love and gratitude, and at the end of the day you will be glad you took a few minutes in the morning to state your intent.

Are your days planned to the finest detail every day? Is there a purpose behind your plan? Or do you just sail along, sometimes rudderless, and see what happens?

Does it matter which of these you choose? All the finest plans in the world can, and do, go astray. The most intricately developed projects do not always come to fruition as set out. Plan all you want, but if there is no intention to drive it forward you have wasted your time. Intention gets things done. Intention leads into commitment and builds into action. Action not words. Heard that before? As in your physical life, so too in your spiritual quest. They say a journey of a thousand miles begins with one small step, but it is intent that starts the whole process.

Have all the goals you want, write down what it is you want, set out where you want to go, but it is all nothing if you have no intention of finishing the job. What do you want to achieve today? How will you achieve it? Do you have the intention to do it? Only you know. Only you can do it. If others are involved how will you be sure if they are committed?

Your life is no accident. You intended it. Long ago you decided to incarnate. Having done that, and come into a physical world you find there are many distractions. What was your original purpose in reincarnating? If you have forgotten the answer then you need to ask your Higher Self. Your Inner Being will tell you. It may not be an instant answer, but if you keep up a conversation with it on a regular basis you will find out more and more about yourself and why you are here. You can then see if you are carrying out your intent or if you have been distracted.

Will you want to return to your birthing intent? Only you can decide. Without intention we are nothing, we achieve nothing. What will you do with yours?

Intention isn't just about activities: it's about emotions and feelings as well.

To what extent do you choose to have positive and loving feelings?

Do you need to change your attitude?

37. Life is like a see saw: it needs both ups and downs.

In order to find balance you have to experience extremes. This is part of your learning and growth. You learn from all situations and experiences. You need the events you term good to experience joy, you need the difficult experiences to learn trust, and to show love for every one and every thing.

When life seems to get you down stop and go into the quiet to find balance within yourself. Ask for guidance to work your way through whatever is present, and know that with love and trust you will succeed. You can't fully appreciate the good times and the gifts you have if that is what you experience all the time.

Don't let the downs get you down mentally and emotionally. Rise up spiritually, know that there is a purpose in all things, and you will find balance and harmony to enable you to move forward.

This is a statement of finding balance. It is a statement of polarity. Always you should be looking for balance and harmony, but how will you know when you have found it? The see-saw moves from one extreme to the other. It has a predetermined high and low and it operates round the balance point.

Life is like that too. It has its very good moments and its terrible moments. By knowing what each is you will know balance when you find it. The extremes define the middle. The extremes will teach you lessons, so look for them. Every event, every situation has a story to tell you. It may not be obvious, it may be obscured, but always it is there. Look for it and learn.

As you strive for balance be aware that you need your ups and downs. Be aware also that the best ride on the see-saw is when it never reaches the full extent of the extremes. It is best when you only move slightly away from the central point. Too rough a ride can see you thrown off, particularly at the top when you are supposed to be on a high.

Life, like the see-saw, is best when the ride is smooth. The ups are good and the downs are manageable without being serious. Life cannot be all one thing. It needs variety, it needs balance. Look for the lessons in each life event and learn from them. That way your see-saw ride will be enjoyable.

Every event, every situation has a story to tell you.

Examine a difficult past event. Consider what lessons were being presented. Did you learn or did you miss the opportunity?

In which parts of your life are you out of balance?

38. A calm pond gives clear reflections. How is your pond?

We have all seen a pond on a sunny day when there are no strong winds, and there is a beautiful reflection of the surrounding landscape. It is almost like a photograph with all the colours of nature. This is so different to a stormy day when the water is rough, and there is no such reflection to be seen.

The mind can be likened to a pond. When the mind is active thoughts go round and round like the water in the pond in stormy weather. With the mind in this state of turmoil it is impossible to link with the Higher Realms, and no guidance can be given.

Allow time each day for the thought process to slow down. When you achieve this meditative state the mind becomes clear, and can reflect what your Higher Self is wishing to communicate. Allow your mind to reflect spirit: do not worry and despair. By allowing your mind to reflect beauty and love you will achieve so much more which will benefit you and others.

Still water will reflect what's around it. By looking at its surface you can see the mirror image of all that borders it. Sometimes it is hard to tell which is real and which is reflection. Can you see what is happening in your world, your pond, if you are not calm?

It is difficult to get the full or true picture when there are disturbances on the surface. You see only snippets, pieces, and they are disjointed. In such conditions it is easy to tell that the reflection is not very accurate.

Being calm means being in control of your thoughts, words and deeds. In such a state you can sense that all is well. You know there is nothing to worry about. You have trusted and it is well founded.

Being calm means your Higher Self is guiding you. When you lose that calmness you have given over to Ego, and you can be misguided. Like the calm surface on the water you can see everything clearly around you when you, too, are calm.

However, still water can become stagnant, and so you must keep moving your pond to avoid this happening to you. You must always be looking to move forward, and thus keep your pond moving. In reality if you look at a calm surface there will be small ripples of movement across it.

Be like the water, stay calm, but be on the move at the same time. Gently does it. No need to make great waves, for that distorts everything. Little by little is the key.

Take small steps with your Higher Self in control, and when you look from the distance, as you should when reviewing yourself, you will see the calm surface and the vivid reflections, knowing that, at a deeper level, there is much going on in a controlled manner.

Allow your mind to reflect spirit.

Taking time to practise slowing down the thought process is important. It's not easy, but, with perseverance, the rewards are worthwhile.

How committed are you to carrying this out?

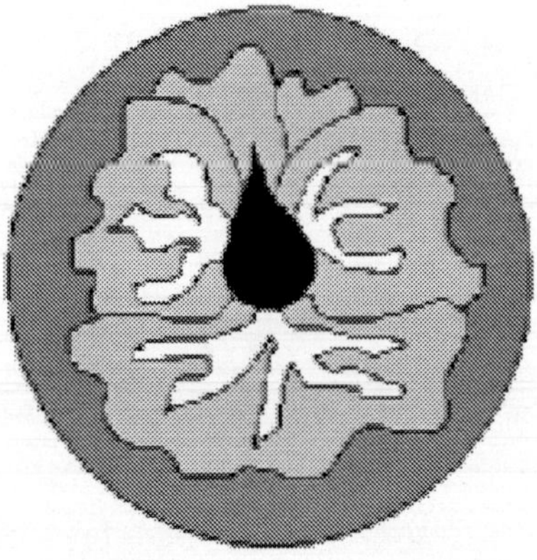

39. Make today a special day because once it has gone you can't relive it.

Many people spend so much of their time going over past events which they wish they could change. It's such a waste of time as they cannot alter what has gone. All they can do is send love to whatever is causing them grief and move into the present. Unfortunately these negative experiences are rarely dealt with in the right way, and can cause problems for years after they occurred.

Take time each day to ensure you live it as you'd really like so that you have no regrets at a later date. Start each day in the right way by connecting with your Higher Self, and asking for guidance and protection no matter what is in store for you throughout the day. Decide that you will endeavour to bring love and light to all people and situations that confront you. Every day is special in that it brings you just the right experiences for your spiritual growth. What more can you ask for? Respond to everything with love, and your loving intentions will ensure that everything happens in the right way. See everyone as special, and know that what they bring you is special even if at first you doubt it.

Go through the day with a positive attitude, and when tomorrow comes you will be able to say that yesterday was indeed a special day.

How many times have you wished you could turn back the clock or go back in time in order to do something differently? However many times you have thought this, you will always realise that it is impossible. In most of life we get only one chance. Thoughts you have, words you say, actions you carry out: there is only one take. You cannot go back and do it again and again until it is perfect.

Many live a life of regret for past actions, words, and thoughts, but we cannot undo them. We can only apologise, ask for forgiveness and learn.

Every situation we get involved in is there to teach us something, and to give us the opportunity to learn the lessons from past events that did not go quite right. We cannot change the past, only learn from it.

Every day you will encounter new situations. How you deal with them will show you how you are progressing as a person, as a spiritual being. Take the chance to move forward, for every time you have regrets you are anchoring yourself to something you can't change.

You need to look at what goes wrong, and make adjustments to ensure it doesn't happen again. Keep a journal of each day and see what life is telling you. By reviewing it on a regular basis you will see if you are progressing.

Each and every day is a new opportunity for you. Grasp it with joy and a sense of wellbeing. See it for what it is: a special opportunity for your development. Live each day to the full. Live each day as it comes. You can't do anything to change the past although you can learn from it, so there is no good in worrying about it. Tomorrow is another day that will unfold in due course, so there is no need to worry about that either. The only day that is important is today so make it very special.

Take time each day to ensure you live it as you'd really like.

How do you ensure you will have no regrets at the end of the day?

Do you ever greet the day as you wake up?

What makes a day special for you?

40. A gift from the heart brings joy to the giver as well as to the receiver

When you give something or do something for someone do it with love and without looking for anything in return. Operate from the heart and not from the Ego. Do not give because it looks good or because you feel that it is your duty to do so. If you do this you are sending out negative energies. Doing something with a grudge does not bring joy to either you or the recipient.

The act of giving should be a pleasure and give you an inward knowing that you are bringing joy to someone else whilst keeping energy flowing. Others can sense when a gift is given grudgingly.

Do not think about what you ought to give, but about what you are able to give without any conditions attached.

If you operate from the heart you will know when it is right to give to others. You will know you are being of service to others, and that you are working on a spiritual and not a material level.

Be open to receiving from others, and appreciate whatever they give you. This can be a present, assistance with a task or simply time to talk or listen. Appreciate what you receive, give thanks to the giver and to the Universe for meeting your needs.

When giving and receiving come from the heart balance is achieved and positive energies are released.

When you give, it should be wholeheartedly, for there is no other way to give. Give from your heart, the centre of your Being and you will experience the joy. Give because you want to, freely and with no conditions or resentments attached.

Be assured whatever you give out will return to you greatly enhanced. As you give freely you will know the joy. So too will the receiver feel that joy, and return it to you along with their joy. They will know that you have given truly with love, and it will show in their reactions.

There is no point in giving grudgingly because, if so, you haven't really given at all. There is no point in counting the cost for that shows that you are not making the gift freely. What you give out, and how you do it, will, in some way, return to you. If you really don't want to give, then don't. It is better not to give than spend time in regret.

In any case you don't have to buy expensive gifts to experience joy. Simple is often best, especially when it is accompanied by love, happiness and warmth. When you give from the heart you give of yourself, and no one can put any monetary value on it.

Those who expect or demand expensive gifts do not understand the true meaning of giving and receiving, and are interested only in shallow material matters. When you are given a gift how do you react? Do you smile and say thank you on the outside but seethe with rage on the inside because it doesn't match your expectation(s)? Do you ever wonder how the gift was given? After all, the gift is only the token. You should be looking at the wider aspects.

If the gift is given with love from the heart, then you can ask no more because the giver has passed their joy to you, and you too should be joyous and return the joy. If we all give from the heart in everything we do we ensure that positive energies circulate round the Universe.

Operate from the heart and not from the Ego.

Think about gifts you can give others that cost nothing in monetary terms but which will light up their life.

41. Don't stumble in the dark when you can switch on the light

So many people stumble around in the darkness going from one difficulty to another without achieving anything. They suffer much and fear there is no hope of improvement. The frame of mind remains negative, attracting more problems and more fear. Answers can't be found as the darkness is intense. It is impossible to think straight and hope is lost. Problems can snowball and seem insurmountable. At least that is what the state of mind suggests. It is easy to become a victim with the "poor me" attitude.

We say attitude is the key to the situation. All it takes is a few moments of time, will power and a determination to change one's outlook. In these few moments switch off from the darkness and raise up your thoughts to the realms of light. Trust that in the light you will be able to cope with whatever tests or lessons you have to face. Realise that in the light you are in contact with your Higher Self, Angels and Beings of Light who wait to assist you. Have the courage to trust them all, knowing that everything happens for a reason. When you focus on the light you will be enlightened, and have a new understanding of your situations. You will welcome whatever comes, knowing that by changing your attitude and emotions you will be able to come out of situations a much stronger and more loving person.

Fill yourself with light, positive thoughts and trust. Light will not take away your difficulties but you will see them in a different way, not as insurmountable problems but as challenges which, when overcome, will assist your spiritual progression.

Switch from thoughts of darkness to thoughts of light, and you will see clearly as to the right pathway for peace and joy.

Remember trees don't grow in the darkness: they strive for the light in order to flourish.

Darkness has the effect of shutting you off from your surroundings. It leaves you with no guiding light or reference points. There is an almost certain effect that you will bump into an object.

It causes you to be extra careful. It can cause you to be still. The alternative is to stumble blindly in some perceived direction without any certainty of a solution. Darkness can be a powerful negative experience.

However, darkness can be a powerful teacher too, and the lessons learned will stand you in good stead. Yes, the darkness can enlighten! A period of darkness should cause you to stand still, or sit down. In this position you are safe. In this position you can take time to work things out and put a plan in place.

A period of personal darkness is best addressed by entering the stillness of your mind and seeking out your Higher Self. By circumventing your Ego you will get an unbiased assessment of your situation. You will get advice on how to deal with whatever has happened. You will get ideas, thoughts, mental pictures.

By discussing your situation with your Higher Self you will be shedding light on your darkness. We know what happens when a light is switched on: everything comes into view, and we can make sense of what we need to do and where we need to go.

Darkness, adversity, crisis, whatever you call it, doesn't come to bring you down, cause worry or depression. It comes to teach. It comes to show you who you really are. Switch on your light and see that person in all their glory.

Attitude is the key.

Are you going through a difficult situation now which could benefit from a change in your attitude towards someone or something?

Have you asked your Higher Self to shed light as to how to deal with it?

42. If you are balanced within, the ups and downs in life won't get you down

If you remain in contact with your Higher Self, receiving guidance and direction in life, you will trust that no matter what, the Universe will take care of you in the right way. You will experience peace within as you will be balanced on all levels, physically, mentally, emotionally and spiritually. You will trust your intuition and have an inner feeling that all will be well.

Life is full of ups and downs, and if everything in our lives went perfectly, with no difficulties, there would be no lessons to learn and our progress would be nil. Earth is a place where we can have many varied experiences which give us an opportunity to show our spiritual qualities.

When upsetting circumstances arise it is all too easy to be thrown off balance and display emotions such as anger, depression, jealousy, to name but a few. We can quickly become disheartened and fear that things will never improve. A negative spiral is invoked and it becomes difficult to see one's way out of a crisis.

However, if we remain balanced we will not swing to any great degree from our centre point. We know that if we remain centred and raise our consciousness upward we will receive insight as to why the difficulty arose, and what we need to learn from it.

We will be in control of our thoughts and emotions, enabling us to think clearly and work towards being able to cope. We learn to understand we may have to make changes, accept others as they are, and even let go of something which we thought was important to us.

The person who is balanced within appreciates the good things in life but knows that these may not last for ever, and that, no matter what happens, they cannot be thrown off course by extremes of circumstances.

As above, so below. As within, so without. Reflections, balance. You have to be sorted out within yourself in order for you to deal with the trials and tests that everyday living will throw at you.

As you are aware, life can take you from one extreme to the other rather like a roller coaster ride. You will be high with elation one minute and the next you will be on a steep slope down until you hit the bottom.

Life can be like this all day, every day, if you are unprepared and cannot deal with it. Exciting it can be, depressing it can also be.

Wouldn't life be easier if you could reduce the height of the high points and reduce the depth of the low points. That way your ride would be smoother with fewer bumps.

In reality your life is a reflection of what is going on inside your body and mind. A body in turmoil translates into a life in turmoil, whereas a body in tune with itself brings a life that is rewarding and satisfying.

Take a long look in the mirror and write down what you see. What parts need changing? Where within your Being do you need to apply the levelling out?

Only you know, but consider areas such as stress levels, anger management, judgmental issues, forgiving and forgetting, love. Where do you stand on these? What do you have to do to bring them into the tolerant range?

Of course your Inner Being, your Higher Self, can help you to identify what needs to be done and can suggest ways in which you may able to bring about change. Do you ever consult your Inner Being?

Do try to make time for yourself to sit in quiet contemplation and open up a conversational channel with your Inner Being. This process can take time to establish, but is worthwhile in its own right.

Taking time just to chill out is often the start of a journey into personal change. However, once you make the connection with your Inner Being the realisation that you are never alone will provide the stimulus for you to continue on your journey.

Once you have started you won't want to stop as you will have discovered that by bringing yourself into balance you are also bringing your everyday life into balance.

We wish you success on your journey.

In reality your life is a reflection of what is going on inside your body and mind.

What changes could you make to achieve balance within in order to create balance in your physical life?

43. Don't bear grudges: put peace in their place

When events don't go as we'd like we often resort to blaming others. We think we are right and they are wrong. We go through emotions of anger and resentment, outraged at injustices; at least that is how we feel it is. Even when the event has long since passed it is easy to hold grudges and go over these events in our minds.

The mind runs riot and we are unable to live in the moment due to focussing on a situation that no longer matters. Grudges pull us back into the past which cannot be changed anyway.

The only positive way to move on is to forgive. If this can be done face to face so much the better, but if this isn't possible, mentally forgive, and send peace and love to those involved.

It is always best to sort out difficulties at the time, but we appreciate this isn't always possible, especially if the other party refuses to communicate.

Remember, you are not responsible for how others think or react. Just because they are unhappy with you doesn't mean you cannot take some action. If you are sorry never be afraid to apologise if this is possible.

In your meditations send love from your heart centre to both the situation and to those involved. Think peace and love instead of negative thoughts. Ask the Universe to bring about peace and harmony.

You will thus have played a positive role in bringing these qualities into the world. You can then move forward knowing you have done your best to resolve the situation.

Remember that what can't be fixed at a physical level can be sorted out at a spiritual level. Forgiveness brings peace, and a peaceful mind allows you to focus on what really matters in the present.

Grudges are indiscretions, wounds, insults from past actions for which you still want revenge. You let the causes of grudges pollute your mind, cloud your judgment and give rise to inappropriate actions.

Your very thoughts, words and deeds are corrupt because you are holding on to a past action which is done and can never be undone. Taken to extremes, the bearing of a grudge can completely mess up the rest of your life as you constantly seek retribution.

The alternative is to put the past where it belongs: behind you. It's gone and there's nothing that anyone can do to make it any different now. Let it go. You have so many more important things to do, like live your life to the fullest capacity.

In letting the past go send love and light to the situation. Try to understand what happened without bias. You will learn something from this, so give thanks to the Universe for this enlightenment. Forgive those involved and replace all the anger with peace.

By doing this you will take away all the negativity and replace it with positive energy. By forgiving from your heart you will be sending love out to the Universe. It will help to heal and seal the wounds you have left open across time.

In yourself you will feel lifted up, as if a great weight has been removed from your shoulders. The red mist of rage that has clouded your eyes will dissipate allowing you to see clearly.

Sending peace back in time allows peace to go out to the Universe and it will return to you. You will find that you will have peace in your heart where anger once ruled. The distortions this caused will be straightened out and you will be able to move on.

Where once anger dominated your life, you will now find yourself ready and able to live in the present and reap the benefits.

The anger that gnawed away at you inside, and perhaps manifested in physical illness, will be gone, and a calmer, happier person will emerge. The peace of the Universe is a wonderful feeling to behold, to be part of. Why be bitter and twisted when you can be at peace with all?

Remember that what can't be fixed at a physical level can be sorted out at a spiritual level.

Do you ask for help from your Higher Self when you feel stuck with no solution?

Have you tried handing your problem over to the Universe and trust that help will be given?

Grudges pull us back into the past which cannot be changed anyway.

Are you holding on to a grudge? If so, examine the negativity you are carrying. Let go and forgive and see the difference it makes.

44. Never interfere with another's journey: you don't know their destination.

It is tempting to become involved in other people's lives and experiences. Sometimes this occurs because we feel we know best and assume we have superior judgments. Other times we become anxious to offer ideas and expect the other party to do as we suggest.

This often happens when we care deeply about someone close to us, as we want to do our best to rescue them from a particular ordeal or relationship. We want to solve their problems and feel they are unable to take the right decisions for themselves.

Never forget we came into an earthly body to experience different pathways and to learn from whatever confronts us.

It is impossible for us to know why another person is going through a particular condition but we can be certain there is a reason for it. If we insist on interfering we may deny the other person the opportunity of learning a particular lesson they need in order to grow spiritually.

Always be willing to help when it is requested. Everyone has free will, so do not deny them the chance to exercise this. Encourage others to come to their own solution by going inside themselves and communicating with their Higher Self for guidance.

Even if others have no understanding of their spiritual side much progress can be made if they sit in the quiet and still the mind. This will give them a clearer picture of the situation.

By standing back, ready to give love and support when requested, you will be showing unconditional love which is the greatest gift you can bestow on another.

You are all individual, you are all unique. Although you are all part of the One and are therefore connected, you all have different aims and objectives. Each one of you created a plan for this life before being born into the physical form that now holds you. Every one of you has a spiritual mission, but every mission is different. Your Inner Being, your Higher Self, is the guardian of your mission.

It never forgets why you are here, and is always available as your mentor. By all means you should experience what the physical world has to offer, but you should also remind yourself of your spiritual quest.

It is easy to be deflected from the path you had identified and get lost on your journey. There are many distractions, but these are tests of your resolve to get to where you want to go. Sadly, many never reach their identified destination because of distractions.

Thus it is important that, in maintaining your focus, you do not distract another from theirs. Yes, you must interact, but no, you mustn't direct another. You can offer counsel, you can relate your experiences, you can discuss, but you have no authority over another's spiritual quest. You have no responsibility for another's spiritual journey, only your own.

Since you have no direct or indirect communication with another's Higher Self you cannot possibly know where they are headed or what experiences they need to acquire. Therefore you should refrain from assumption, and from passing judgment on them.

As has been said, discuss with another their journey, but if they truly need help then they must, as everyone else must, communicate with their Higher Self. This is the only place, the only Source, where they can be truly and honestly advised. Then, like everyone else, they use their own judgment and free will to move on.

Your journey is your own. Your friend's journey is theirs. Let's agree to keep them separate.

You have no responsibility for another's spiritual journey.

Do you get upset when someone you love rejects your advice?

How do you react?

What adjustments do you need to make in order to respond lovingly and accept their free will?

What stops you from letting go of your desire to exert control over another?

How do you feel when someone tries to exert control over your decisions and actions?

45. A river is fed from its source: where does your nourishment come from?

A river which starts as a small spring from the earth begins to flow, and as it does, it gets wider and wider. However, no matter how far the river continues it will always be fed from its source. Water may come from other means such as rainfall but the river will always be connected and nourished from where it began.

Never forget your own connection to Source or God. This is your origin and you are connected for infinity to Source: you are part of it.

Whilst in a physical body going through your journey on Earth you are always connected to your spiritual body even if you do not realise it. The river is always connected to its source and so are you. In fact, you and the river have the same greater Source which is God, or the Universe, whichever way you wish to look at it.

It is important to nourish your physical body, giving it the right amounts of healthy food and water. It is all too easy to forget that nourishment should also be sought from your spiritual self. By connecting to the Higher Realms you will find what you need to complement your physical nourishment. You will find peace, healing, solutions to your problems and an inner knowing that if you trust Source all will be right for you. Your physical, mental, and emotional bodies will be nourished by your spirit and all your bodies will be aligned and balanced. You can then flow with ease through life just as the river flows naturally from its source to the sea.

The river starts from a tiny trickle and can end up as an enormous watery artery containing millions upon millions of gallons of water. On its way from its source, throughout its journey, it may also be fed by other streams or it may indeed itself flow into a still greater river: it can do both.

What about you? You too have a Source, you too have a journey, and you too interact with others. However, your needs and nourishment are far more complex than the river's, but you can still learn from how the river grows.

In the physical world you get distracted by many things: there is diversity in life, and it diverts you from your path. You can get led away from your purpose and dry up: your nourishment gone. You can come up against insurmountable objects, be held back and become stagnant. You can get caught up in another's journey and lose your identity: similarly others can get caught up in your journey, and you become a wild raging torrent capable of destroying anything in your path.

If you are to avoid these things then you must remember your Source and keep in mind your goal. You need to remember that you are a spiritual being in a physical world looking to gain the right experiences to further your mission.

That is not to say that such experiences as outlined above cannot be part of your spiritual mission: perhaps you need to experience such aspects so that you can understand balance. After all, how do you know cold if you do not experience hot?

By remembering Source and goal you stay on your path. By communicating with Source and discussing goals you remain focussed and guided. This will help you when obstacles appear: you will be able to cope, and find the way past them.

You, like the river, are nourished from Source and whatever your goal, you will reach it so long as you keep Source close to you.

Never forget your own connection to Source or God.

Do you find it hard to remember your connection to Source when things go wrong?

If you connect daily you will find you automatically ask for help in both good and bad times.

46. Amid noise you can still find peace. In nothingness you can find everything

Everyday life on Earth can often be filled with noise of all kinds. This can cause stress, and the rushing around takes its toll on the body. There never seems to be time to switch off, but it is important to allocate time for this. Even a short period of meditation twice a day can be of enormous benefit.

It is best to start practising meditation when all is quiet as it is easier to still the mind when there are no distractions. With everyday practice it will eventually be possible to still the mind when confronted by external noise. Many people find they can use time whilst travelling on buses and trains to go within, and find peace and calm.

When the mind is still and thoughts are not running riot it is then possible to connect with your Higher Self and guidance can be received. With turmoil gone from the mind, there is space to receive the help you require. A mind filled with worries and problems has no room for valuable input from Spirit.

Start the day by being still and peaceful. Once you start your daily activities, even although there is chaos and noise around you, you can remind yourself to adopt that feeling of calmness and serenity. You don't have to be part of the hustle and bustle around you. You can be in control of your state of mind. Take control of how you want to be, and let others react in whatever way is right for them.

The more you practise being peaceful when all is quiet, the better able you will be to cope with whatever you have to face during day to day activities.

There is always noise around us: we call it background noise. There is never an absolute silence, which would probably drive us insane. Amid this background noise we can still perform our everyday tasks and activities. We do them without thinking about the various noises in the background at the perimeter of our hearing.

Noise does not detract from our concentration or understanding nor does it inhibit us so long as it is at a low level. Some even prefer noise to assist them in what they do.

No matter where we go or what we do there is always noise. Yet amidst this we can still find peace. We can sit amid the noise and focus inwards, shutting off the noise from our senses. As we concentrate on going inwards the noise fades from our consciousness, and we reach peace. We reach that wonderful stillness of inner calm.

This is where our Higher Self resides and we can communicate silently but meaningfully with our Inner Being. We can open up our worries and problems to our Inner Self, and in return we listen for the answers coming back. We hear the truth, we see alternatives: we are reminded of who we really are, and what our journey is.

When our worries are taken care of and our fears are lessened we can begin to straighten out the twisted, and our vision clears. In the nothingness that exists when we communicate with our Higher Self we find everything we need. Abundance is truly ours. Help is at hand. Comfort and joy are experienced.

Whatever our problems, whatever our worries, we should actively seek out that silence amidst the noise. When we have found it we have found everything. As if from nowhere the answers are there, inside you, waiting for you. Shut out the noise and see what you find.

A mind filled with worries and problems has no room for valuable input from spirit.

You may have no control over your surroundings but you can learn to exercise control of your mind. Practice makes perfect.

What excuses do you make when you don't set aside time for daily meditations? Do you need to re-prioritise your daily activities?

47. Choose your thoughts as carefully as you choose your words

Many people are aware that they should be careful in what they say to others. They realise that words said in anger may cause upset for many years to come, as what's said cannot be unsaid. Something said without thinking can cause hurt and anger, resulting in bad feelings, and forgiveness may never come even after apologies are given.

Whilst we advise you to think before you speak harsh words, we would like to emphasise the amount of harm which comes from impure thoughts, even although these are not expressed verbally to another person. As we have said before, thoughts are energy and negative thoughts will reach others and may cause them to suffer if they do not protect themselves with light.

There is no point in being nice to someone whilst having thoughts which don't match what you say. The negative thoughts you give out will return to you at some time in the future. So give out only that which you would like to receive.

Any thoughts which come to mind that you realise are not spiritual, can be cancelled mentally and you can replace them with positive thoughts, feelings or affirmations. Be constantly monitoring your thoughts, have control over them and see the positive change in your life.

Just because others cannot read your thoughts doesn't mean these thoughts have no significance. Let your thoughts match your words and let them all be loving.

Everyone has their own reality, therefore we see things differently. We each create a reality that is unique, because it belongs to us and no one else. Yes, there are aspects of our realities that overlap and that is what allows us to communicate, one with another.

We communicate most often by word: whether spoken or written. That is why we should choose words carefully. If we don't then there is a very good possibility that misunderstandings will occur.

If we are trying to convey our reality to another we have to be very specific in our description otherwise the other person will see it differently, and we will be communicating at cross purposes. We should always check frequently that we have understood, and are understood by others.

However, behind every word we utter or write is a thought. Thoughts are the spark of our reality, and from them come our words and our actions. Thoughts define our reality.

It is therefore essential that we control our thoughts, for, if one escapes before we have it under control, who can tell what damage can be wreaked upon another person.

If we are treading the spiritual path we should be thinking only positive thoughts. We should be looking for the best in others as well as in ourselves. Positive thoughts engender a positive outlook, and that leads to a positive attitude. We will therefore think our way into looking for the best in our life. We will see the best in others. We will see the message when events don't go as well as we would have liked.

Positive thinking means we will learn from everything we do. Positive thinking means we will use only the most appropriate words. Positive thinking means our actions will be for the good of everyone.

Choose your thoughts carefully: your reality depends on them.

Thoughts define our reality.

Are you always sincere with your thoughts? Do they match what you say and do?

Remember how powerful thoughts are and this should assist you in taking care that they are positive and loving.

48. Getting to know yourself isn't easy but the rewards are great

Getting to know yourself takes a lifetime as you keep changing. Your thoughts and ideas change as you grow older, and even a few years bring changes in outlook and beliefs.

Often people do not take the time to examine who they really are and get to know what makes them tick. We have all been influenced by others in our lives and taken on their values without challenging them. Very often we carry grudges, and behave in certain ways without realising why.

It takes time and effort to really understand and get to know oneself. Making the acquaintance of one's Inner Child can help us realise how much we are affected in adulthood by events and relationships in childhood.

By connecting daily with our Higher Self we get to know more about our true Self and what we planned for this lifetime prior to incarnating in our physical body. We all came with a life plan but unless we take time to connect with our Higher Self we may never realise what we intended to accomplish.

When we fully understand that we are spiritual beings in a physical body we can have more fulfilled lives, and find harmony within ourselves.

As we get to know and understand ourselves better we realise we have lessons to learn. Instead of fighting an inner battle when things go wrong we can accept mistakes, learn from them and move on. We recognise that others go through difficult times as well, and we become more tolerant and patient with them. As we accept our own mistakes and learn to love ourselves we become more loving and forgiving towards others.

Everything worthwhile requires time and effort, and with learning to value and love yourself you will find you are not just at one with yourself but with all creation.

You are a complex being, and that's just at the physical level! The way in which your physical body works to keep all of its systems just so is quite remarkable. However, these words are not about your physical make up or operation.

Your mind is certainly the most complex thing you will ever encounter. How it works, or why, has defied investigation for countless years.

Why do you react as you do? Why do you like or dislike? Why do you rush to snap judgments? Do you ever wonder or just accept it as the way you are?

Is how you interact with society really "you"? Do you deliver the real you to the world, or is what the world sees merely a charade? A show put on for whatever reason?

What do you get out of putting on a show? Does it make you feel good? Are you trying to gain friends and create a good impression on others? What kind of world do you operate in? Are you happy with the person you portray yourself to be?

If you are happy with the personality you project then well done. However, if you are not then don't despair. Help is always at hand if you only realised it.

To gain maximum help you need to find out who you really are. This requires a journey inwards, to your very Soul. Deep inside each one of us is our Inner Being, our Higher Self. That part of us which knows who we are, why we came into being, and where we stand in relation to the goals we set.

Our Higher Self waits patiently for communication. We can do so by focussing inwards. It may take time and several attempts, but persistence will be rewarded. The key to it all is to bypass Ego, for Ego is the part of us that is pushing us in the wrong direction. Once Ego is out of the way you will be able to communicate with your Higher Self and be told all those things that you had forgotten about yourself, those things that Ego had persuaded you to forget.

You will discover your spiritual reality and life plan. You will gain insight on all fronts. You will see who you really are. There will be many questions to resolve, and dilemmas to ponder over.

However, you will have the choice of what to do, because you have free will. You will have the understanding of what you wanted to experience, what you wanted to achieve. You will have the knowledge of how you are currently living your life, of how you are expressing yourself to the world.

It is up to you whether you want to continue as you are or whether you want to make changes. It's your free will, it's your life. If you make the effort to know yourself the Universe will reward you by giving you the answers. Whatever direction you now choose, the decision will have been based on knowing all the facts and will, therefore, be in everyone's best interests.

Is how you interact with society really "you"?

Do you find yourself doing things for the wrong reasons?

Do you exercise your free will?

Do you really know your true self?

Is it time to change and be yourself?

What was the last thing you did because you wanted to and not because of pressure or influence from others?

49. Have peace in your thoughts and this is what the world will reflect back to you

Thoughts create reality and by being in control of your thoughts your reality will be as you would like. It is easy to let your thoughts run riot and if something annoys you many negative thoughts run through your mind: this only adds to whatever negativity there already is.

It's not easy to control thoughts, especially if this is something new to you, but it gets easier the more you practise. Take time to monitor your thoughts, and if you don't like those that come to mind substitute them with what you feel would be more appropriate. It helps to change your attitude, and if you adopt a loving attitude, looking for a positive quality in everyone and everything, then your thoughts will also be peaceful and loving.

If you accept that all life is one and part of Source then you will find it easier to be at peace with all creation. You will know that nothing happens by chance and that all things fit together like a jigsaw puzzle. It may not be obvious at the time, but when you look back at a later stage you will see more parts of the picture.

If you are at peace within yourself your peaceful thoughts will be projected out to all around, and this is what will come back to you. The more you practise this, the more you will find it to be true. You have to work at it, but the rewards are great.

When you are at peace within, your physical body benefits as well as your emotional and mental bodies. If you feel you have to say something which another person may not want to hear do it with love and a desire to make peace between you. Think peace, experience peace, radiate peace and the world will be a better place.

You are a microcosm of all that happens and is happening. Your thoughts create your reality and that interacts with everyone else's reality. In general terms our realities overlap almost seamlessly, but there are times and places when disputes and disagreements occur.

It is perhaps inevitable that we experience little rough patches, but we can minimise them. If your life is one long rough patch then something major has gone wrong with your reality creating mechanism. What exactly are your thoughts? Do you harbour unachievable ambitions? Do you hold on to hurt and insult? Are you seeking revenge for an act that happened a long time ago?

You need to examine your thought pattern and your beliefs. You may need to reassess what it is you want and how you are going to get it. You may need to change.

Undergoing change is not easy but you have to love the person you are or want to be. When you can love yourself you will find that life becomes easier. You should make your changes at a pace you are comfortable with, and enjoy the experience this will bring you.

You will find yourself thinking new thoughts. Thoughts of love, thoughts of appreciation, thoughts of peace. These aspects will manifest in your reality, and will become obvious to others with whom you communicate and interact. As your peaceful thoughts go out into the world they will help to bring peace to situations in which you find yourself. Your world will become more peaceful, and this peace will reflect back to you.

Sending out and getting back peace puts you in a win-win situation. It works also with everything you think, so be careful only to think and send out to the world those thoughts you are happy with. Think carefully and reap the benefits.

Sending out and getting back peace puts you in a win-win situation.

Do you find yourself sending out negative thoughts when on the receiving end of another person's anger?

This cannot be a solution as the situation can only worsen as negativity multiplies. Have the courage to send out love and see the difference.

50. If you have doubts and fears you have lost trust in the Universe

Doubts and fears are blocks you put up which hinder progress. If you fill your mind with negative ideas then this is what you are putting out to the Universe, and this is what will govern your existence. Never forget you create your situations, and attract to you whatever corresponds to your thinking. The Universe will return to you what you give out.

Doubting the Universe is doubting your own creativity, and doubting the help which is available to you. It is doubting God. It is failing to recognise the God within you and all others.

Dispense with doubts and fears. This is not easy to start with. It takes a lot of courage to do so. However, it is the only way forward. Replace despondency with love. Love whatever occurs, trusting that you attracted it as a learning opportunity. Ask for guidance as to why you are faced with the situation, and what part it can play in your development. Believe that there is a reason for everything, and trust that although it may be hard to cope, help and support will be given, provided you ask for it.

Hand over to the Universe whatever is getting you down, trusting that there is a purpose in all things. It may not be in your best interests to see the whole picture, but know that whatever is happening is right for you. If you trust the Angels and Beings of Light you will face everything with love, knowing that your spiritual qualities will see you through. The more you learn to let go and trust, the easier it will become to remain positive at all times.

As you go about your physical life there are services you make use of, and you have to trust that those offering the service will deliver as promised. Sometimes things will go wrong and you may become a little wary when next using that service. This is understandable.

However, you have let doubt into your mind and this can affect all manner of things that you are involved in. The doubt can turn to fear and spread right through your everyday life. Then normal service gets resumed, and everything again becomes all right.

When you go into the quiet and converse with the Universe you are communicating with all of creativity. When you ask the Universe for help you need to maintain your trust that the Universe will be responsive to your needs.

If you express any doubts or fears the Universe will pick up on this, and, as you are aware, will return to you any energies that you send out. If you ask with fear and foreboding you will not get the answer you were perhaps hoping for, but you will get the answer you deserve.

Whereas if you make a request with love and trust, you will have detached yourself from the outcome, and the answer will be the right one for all involved.

Negativity is a powerful destructive force and its consequences are devastating. Negativity will tear apart even the best laid plans. Positivity, on the other hand, is a powerful creative force which can build great structures from small beginnings.

Never lose your trust in the Universe; it will not let you down. When you trust in the Universe, it will return that trust to you. How can you possibly doubt that?

Doubting the Universe is doubting your own creativity.

Is there a situation in your life causing you worry and fear?

Remember your spiritual connection and bring forth your spiritual qualities of unconditional love, joy, forgiveness and trust. Send out these qualities to others and allow these energies to create positive changes for all involved.

Spiritual Growth

When life gets hard
And the going gets tough
And you start to feel
You've had enough.
When all goes wrong
And you want to cry
Then it's time to stop
And wonder why.
You need to take stock
Of what's going on
So take time to be still
Or the day will be gone.
Rise up to the Realms
Of Beauty and Peace
Allowing the turmoil
Around you to cease.
Ask for the guidance
That will help you to cope
Allowing your mind
To be filled with new hope.
Ask for some insight
As to what's going on
And with new understanding
Worries soon will be gone.
You'll know each event
Has some meaning for you
And the higher you rise
The better the view.
You'll welcome what comes
As you'll know it is right
And you'll struggle less
In a fruitless fight.
You'll then be able
To go with the flow
And spiritual growth
You will surely know.

EPILOGUE

SPIRITUAL PROGRESSION

All wisdom is within you. Tap into this in whatever ways are right for you. Do not just use one method as this is restrictive, and a slower progression will result. All roads lead to the Godhead but there are many tools available.

First of all make the time and effort, and be steadfast in your purpose. Know where you want to go and what goal you wish to achieve. Observe yourself as well as others, but remember that they are on their paths with their chosen methods. You have your own preferred ways so use these. Keep an open mind and use whatever methods feel right for you at any given time. Review your situation regularly and be prepared to make changes to suit your needs.

Make every activity a meditation. Observe yourself doing it and ask yourself how you are feeling. See a purpose in all things, even what seems mundane and monotonous. These tasks give you a chance to slow down the mind. You can use affirmations as you do them. Love what you do. That is a meditation in itself.

Know yourself. By keeping a journal you will learn so much about yourself and what works best for you. Again find joy in doing this. It's like writing your own school report. You comment. You see the progress. You plan the next stage of learning. Do not be harsh on yourself or you will stop yourself from moving on.

Do not hold back waiting for perfection. See the opportunities and plan how to make the most of them. You are the student, teacher, inspector all rolled into one. This enables you to take control of your life. Make it fun and joyful, allowing yourself and others to make mistakes. When all is perfect opportunities for progression cannot arise.

Remember to count your blessings, for that is the first step towards feeling joyful and abundant.

A

B

C

E

F

G

H

I

J

M

P

R

S

T

U

V

W

Living the Spiritual Laws
For Health and Abundance

Living the Spiritual Laws gives an easy-to-follow introduction to 36 Spiritual Laws. Each of the two authors has channelled a short explanation of each Law, thus giving a slightly different angle to the interpretation. You are encouraged to meditate and write your own interpretations.

Living the Spiritual Laws is also a self help guide to living the Laws on a day to day basis. Through questions and meditations you will be helped to identify where each Law fits in relation to everyday living.

In *Living the Spiritual Laws* you will be guided to

- incorporate the Laws into your life
- keep a daily journal to record events, your reactions and how you could have responded in a more spiritual way
- construct and use affirmations
- follow the 16 steps to Living the Laws

Living the Spiritual Laws will change your approach to life, empowering you to take control and grow spiritually.

Andrew and Helen are experienced Therapists, Healers and Teachers. They have written and presented their workshops extensively.

During a difficult period in their life they turned to channelling on the Spiritual Laws for help and guidance. The answers they received were put into practice, enabling them to let go of fear and use the situations to grow spiritually. They believe that what they have been given is for sharing with others: service is the pathway to Spiritual Enlightenment.

Available from Well Within Therapies 26 Orchard Road, Kingston upon Thames, KT1 2QW. Price £10 incl postage (UK)

or from your local bookshop, ISBN 0-9545446-0-9.